JUDAISM

A N D

th

Fulfilling the promise of its title, this thoughtful and penetrating book constitutes a meditation on the values of Judaism and the ideals projected by the Declaration of Independence, treating both sets of traditions not in isolation one from the other, but as they intertwine.

Although Milton Konvitz is interested in the questions "What is a Jew?" and "What is an American?" his primary concern, as he states in the introduction, "is not with being but with ideals and values." As he makes clear, there is such a thing as the American-Hebraic Idea, which is manifested in the ideals of human dignity, the Rule of Law, the democratic ideal, the rights of conscience, and the pursuit of happiness.

He addresses his book "to all persons, whatever their religion or nationality." "The ideals presented here," he goes on to say, "are meant to soften boundaries, to mitigate differences, to remove obstacles that stand in the way of those who know that common ideals do exist in this world in which we live and move and have our being."

Grounded firmly in the classic sources of Judaism and in American political theory and development, this book makes an important contribution to both Jewish and American intellectual history. It is certain to appeal to American Jews who are seeking identity as Americans and as Jews, and to any reader interested in understanding why Jews feel rooted in modern America.

Books by Milton R. Konvitz

On the Nature of Value
The Alien and the Asiatic in American Law
The Constitution and Civil Rights
Civil Rights in Immigration
Fundamental Liberties of a Free People: Religion, Speech, Press,
    Assembly
A Century of Civil Rights (with Theodore Leskes)
Expanding Liberties
Religious Liberty and Conscience
Judaism and the American Idea

Editor of

Freedom and Experience (with Sidney Hook)
Essays in Political Theory (with Arthur H. Murphy)
Law and Social Action: Selected Essays of Alexander H. Pekelis
Education for Freedom and Responsibility by Edmund Ezra Day
Liberian Code of Laws
Liberian Code of Laws Revised
Liberian Law Reports
Aspects of Liberty (with Clinton Rossiter)
Bill of Rights Reader: Leading Constitutional Cases
The American Pragmatists (with Gail Kennedy)
Emerson: A Collection of Critical Essays (with Stephen E. Whicher)
First Amendment Freedoms: Selected Cases on Freedom of Religion,
    Speech, Press, Assembly
Judaism and Human Rights
The Recognition of Ralph Waldo Emerson

JUDAISM

AND

the American Idea

Milton R. Konvitz

Cornell University Press

Ithaca and London

First published 1978 by Cornell University Press.
Published in the United Kingdom by Cornell University Press Ltd.,
2-4 Brook Street, London W1Y 1AA.

International Standard Book Number 0-8014-1181-5
Library of Congress Catalog Card Number 78-58028
Printed in the United States of America
*Librarians: Library of Congress cataloging information appears on the last
page of the book.*

❧/ To Eli, my grandson

Who among you, created in the image of God, could compare
himself with his Creator? Yet I say unto you: Even if
the heavens were to descend or the earth to break asunder,
a man must not renounce his rights.

—Menahem Mendel of Kotzk

There is what I call the American idea. I so name it because
it seems to me to lie at the basis of all our truly original,
distinctive, and American institutions. It is itself a complex
idea, composed of three subordinate and more simple ideas,
namely: the idea that all men have unalienable rights; that
in respect thereof, all men are created equal; and that government is to be established and sustained for the purpose of
giving every man an opportunity for the enjoyment and development of all these unalienable rights.

—Theodore Parker

2082084

CONTENTS

PREFACE

THE ESSAYS IN THIS BOOK are written by one who sees himself indissolubly as both an American and a Jew. I could not, for the life of me, ever say where one ends and the other begins. I know, of course, that one can be an American without being a Jew, and that one can be a Jew without being an American. But my concern here is not with being but with ideals and values. Ideals may have their sources in a specific tradition, but their nature is to transcend the limits imposed by time and space, by nations, states, churches, and other institutions. Just as there is an ideal America, so too there is an ideal Judaism; each has shrines at which worship men and women who are neither Americans nor Jews, just as St. Paul's audience at Athens worshiped at an altar dedicated "to an unknown God." The book, then, concerned as it is with human ideals and rights, is addressed to all persons, whatever their religion or nationality. The ideas here presented have as their objective the softening of boundaries, the mitigation of differences, the removal of obstacles that stand in the way of those who know that common ideals do exist in this complex world in which we live and move and have our being.

Five of the eight essays were prepared in celebration of the American Bicentennial. Three other essays, published previously, are so germane to the intertwining relationship of Judaism and the American Idea that they may be fittingly appropriated to the book.

During the academic year 1975–1976 I enjoyed the privilege of a senior fellowship of the National Endowment for the Humanities, which made possible the writing of a major part of this book. I am, of course, grateful for the opportunity that this support allowed me.

M. R. K.

Ithaca, New York

ACKNOWLEDGMENTS

"Human Dignity—from Creation to Constitution" appeared in somewhat different form in *The 70th Anniversary of The Dropsie University* (Philadelphia, 1978), a volume published by The Dropsie University to honor the memory of Professor Solomon Zeitlin.

An earlier version of "The Rule of Law: Torah and Constitution" was published in the *Rabbinical Assembly Proceedings* for 1976 (New York: Rabbinical Assembly, 1977).

"Judaism and the Democratic Ideal" was originally a chapter in *The Jews: Their Religion and Culture*, edited by Louis Finkelstein (New York: Harper & Row, 1949; copyright © by Louis Finkelstein, 1949, 1955, 1960, 1971), and is revised for this book.

"Conscience: Movement from Duty to Right—from Bible to Bill of Rights" appeared, in part, in *Of Law and Man: Essays in Honor of Haim H. Cohn*, edited by Shlomo Shoham (New York and Tel Aviv: Sabra Books, 1971), and in part as an article in *The Hastings Law Journal* (Hastings College of the Law, University of California, 1978).

"Individual Conscience or Group Consciousness—Religious Liberty in Israel and the United States," several times revised, was presented as the Israel Goldstein Annual Lecture at the Hebrew University and was published as a pamphlet by the Institute of Contemporary Jewry, Hebrew University, 1971, and as an article in the magazine *Judaism*, Spring issue, 1971.

"From Jewish Rights to Human Rights" appeared in an earlier version in *Human Rights: Aspects of the Jewish Experience*, edited by David Sidorsky (Philadelphia: The Jewish Publication Society, 1978).

"Life and Liberty for the Pursuit of Happiness," first given in another version as the Sol Feinstone Lecture at the Jewish Theological Seminary, was published by the Seminary as a pamphlet in 1977.

Permission to use copyrighted materials was granted in each case, and such permission is gratefully acknowledged to Harper & Row, The Dropsie University, The Jewish Publication Society, the periodical *Judaism*, the Rabbinical Assembly, Sabra Books, *The Hastings Law Journal*, and the Jewish Theological Seminary.

JUDAISM

AND

the American Idea

INTRODUCTION:

The American-Hebraic Idea

I

ON A RAINY SUNDAY in July 1848, on Emerson's second visit to England, Emerson and Carlyle found themselves at the home of friends at Bishops Waltham. At one point in the conversation, Emerson relates,

> my friends asked, whether there were any Americans?—any with an American idea,—any theory of the right future of that country? Thus challenged, I bethought myself neither of caucuses nor congress, neither of presidents nor of cabinet-ministers, nor of such as would make of America another Europe. I thought only of the simplest and purest minds; I said, "Certainly yes;—but those who hold it are fanatics of a dream which I should hardly care to relate to your English ears, to which it might be only ridiculous,—and yet it is the only true [idea]."[1]

What Emerson tried to say to his English friends was that there was, indeed, an "American idea," something that transcended institutional devices, something that was ideal and spiritual, something religious, something that could be expressed only, or best, he said, in terms of "the law of love and justice."

It was not until 1856, eight years later, that Emerson published *English Traits*, which recorded the conversation with his English friends. Meantime, however, in 1850, Theodore Parker, speaking at an abolitionist meeting in Boston, used the phrase "the America idea" as one in which religion, political philosophy, and governmental institutions converged. "There is," said Parker, "what I call the American idea."

I so name it because it seems to me to lie at the basis of all our truly original, distinctive, and American institutions. It is itself a complex idea, composed of three subordinate and more simple ideas, namely: the idea that all men have unalienable rights; that in respect thereof, all men are created equal; and that government is to be established and sustained for the purpose of giving every man an opportunity for the enjoyment and development of all these unalienable rights. This idea demands, as the proximate organization thereof, a democracy, that is, a government of all the people, by all the people, for all the people;[2] of course, a government after the principles of eternal justice, the unchanging law of God. . . .[3]

This is the American idea which is the background of my book and which is its essence. It is the text on which the book is commentary: the idea of inalienable rights, the equality of all human beings, equality of opportunity, a true democracy, the law of justice, the law of love, the law of God; the near and the far, the dream and the operative principles, the short view and the long view of things; the union of political theory and religious ideals.

"Why is it, do you suppose," E. B. White asks, "that an Englishman is unhappy until he has explained America . . . but one seldom meets an American who is all tensed up because he has yet to explain England?"[4] Emerson did not think of asking Carlyle or any of his other English friends whether there were any *Englishmen*—any with an *English* idea—any theory of the right future of *that* country? He did not find it at all strange that his English friends should challenge him to justify his existence as an *American*. After two hundred years of independence the situation has hardly changed. Who would think of asking a Frenchman what is "the French idea"—or asking what is "the Italian idea," or "the Brazilian idea," or "the Turkish idea"? Old nations and young are simply taken for granted—Greece and India, Burundi and Barbados—as facts of life. Just as one would not think of looking for a reason for the existence of the elephant or the chipmunk, so one does not ask for the reason that would explain the existence of Albanians or Russians.

But there are two exceptions: the Jewish people and the Americans. For thousands of years the world has challenged the right of the Jews to their own national existence, and in one world forum or another the question persists, as if the world can find no rest until the issue is satisfactorily resolved. The situation is different for Americans, whose national existence is taken for granted. In this respect Americans are not different from Englishmen or Frenchmen. But the reasons for the existence of the American nation still excite interest. The concern is with the Platonic Idea of the American nation in its perfection, or with the Aristotelian Final Cause; that is, with the purpose or function of the American nation, the end which it is intended to serve or achieve. There is always the quest for the teleological explanation, for the moral meaning of being an American.

It is not only Carlyle who asks Emerson to tell him what is the American idea; Americans have always, from the very beginning, asked themselves the same question. The Pilgrims, sailing from Plymouth in 1620, entered into the Mayflower Compact, the wording of which makes clear that the Pilgrim leaders conceived of their new civil polity as merely an extension of a church covenant. By the Compact they promised one another that they would enact only "such just and equal laws, Ordinances, Acts, Constitutions, and Offices" as shall order, preserve and further the glory of God, the advancement of the Christian faith, the honor of King and country, and the general good of the colony. It was for these ends, held consciously before their minds, that they constituted themselves "a civil Body Politick."[5] Unlike their relatives and friends who remained at home in England, and who could go on being Englishmen as roses go on being roses, the Pilgrims could become Americans only by projecting the idea of an America as a sort of Final Cause which would explain why it was that they had left home to make for themselves a new home and themselves into a new nation.

In his essay "The Gods of the Nations and God," Martin Buber refines and develops an idea Nachman Krochmal took from Giambattista Vico—the idea that every nation elevates itself as its absolute principle; its own national existence becomes the god it worships—it knows no higher principle than that. But Israel is an exception: it does not place its own national existence as the ultimate absolute. Instead, "Israel experiences the absolute as that which Israel itself is not and which it can never become, and reveres it as such. Or to put it differently: the nations can experience the absolute only because of what they are; Israel can experience the absolute only, when, and because that absolute faces it."[6] Israel knows only one absolute: "Israel knows only one God, the Eternal."[7]

America, from the time of its very founding, has tended to see itself as a kind of New Israel, planted, under God's providential guidance, in a New World. In the eighteenth century, however, when the Declaration of Independence and the Constitution came to be written, the strong influence of the Enlightenment led Franklin, Washington, Jefferson, Madison, and other leaders of American thought to speak rather of "the Laws of Nature and of Nature's God," and of certain "self-evident" truths and of certain "unalienable Rights," including "Life, Liberty, and the pursuit of Happiness."[8] These became the absolutes for Americans, and on the whole have remained such. Essentially they became the essence of the American idea as it was seen by Theodore Parker and Ralph Waldo Emerson; and while these words and phrases are not to be found in the written Constitution, they are, as it were, the "oral Constitution" without which the written words can hardly be understood.

II

We might remind ourselves that it was precisely this claim of uniqueness that Walt Whitman made for America in his *Democratic Vistas*, written just five years before the first American Centennial Celebration.

For our New World I consider far less important for what it has done, or what it is, than for results to come. *Sole among nationalities, these States have assumed the task to put in form of lasting power and practicality, on areas of amplitude rivaling the operations of the physical kosmos, the more political speculations of ages*, long, long deferred, the democratic republican principle, and the theory of development and perfection by voluntary standards, and self-reliance. *Who else, indeed, except the United States, in history, so far, have accepted in unwitting faith, and, as we now see, stand, act upon, and go security for, these things?* [9]

What the nation needed, Whitman wrote, was a class of teachers, schools, and poets who would unveil the "religious and moral character beneath the political and productive and intellectual bases" of the United States.[10] For, he believed, underlying all appearances and unconscious strivings, there was a "fervid and tremendous Idea"[11] that far transcended our politics, our laws, our material objects, our physical plenty and industry.

But, wrote Whitman, there must be no delusion that the lives of the American people, at the time of the first American Centennial, already manifested the "fervid and tremendous Idea." As he looked about him, he saw everywhere corruption: the government, in all its branches and departments, except the judiciary, were "saturated in corruption, bribery, falsehood, maladministration"; and the courts, while not corrupt, were "tainted." And the cities of America "reek with respectable as much as non-respectable robbery and scoundrelism." Money-making was "the sole master of the field."[12]

Whitman, however, was not a thinker who tended to under-
value the material aspects of life; "matter" was not a dirty word
in his vocabulary. The ideal democracy that he projected, he
said, "looks with suspicious, ill-satisfied eye upon the very poor,
the ignorant, and those out of business. She asks for men and
women with occupations, well-off, owners of houses and acres,
and with cash in the bank." The model he had in mind had, he
said, "a practical, stirring, worldly, money-making, even mate-
rialistic character."

I perceive clearly that the extreme business energy, and this almost
maniacal appetite for wealth prevalent in the United States, are parts
of amelioration and progress, indispensably needed to prepare the
very results I demand. My theory includes riches, and the getting of
riches, and the amplest products, power, activity, inventions, movements, etc. Upon them, as upon sub-strata [the fervid and tremendous Idea], I raise the edifice designed in these [*Democratic*] *Vistas.*
. . .[13] I hail with joy the oceanic, variegated, intense practical energy, the demand for facts, even the business materialism of the current age, our States. But woe to the age and land in which these
things, movements, stopping at themselves, do not tend to ideas. As
fuel to flame, and flame to the heavens, so must wealth, science,
materialism—even this democracy of which we make so much—un-
erringly feed the highest mind, the soul. Infinitude the flight: fa-
thomless the mystery. Man, so diminutive, dilates beyond the sensi-
ble universe, competes with, outcopes space and time, meditating
even one great idea.[14]

When Whitman tried to give some content to the "tremendous
Idea" that America was to represent and fulfill, he could only
fall back upon Biblical language: "By the names right, justice,
truth, we suggest, but do not describe it."[15] He had in mind, he
wrote, America's "moral civilization," its expression of "absolute Conscience, moral soundness, Justice."[16] These are the
"ever-overarching American ideas."[17] This, he said, is "the
American program, not for classes, but for universal man,"
embodied in the Declaration of Independence and in the Constitution with its amendments.

Now, then, Whitman reasoned, we have reached two of the

necessary stages: we have projected our "American program," and we have built up the material base necessary for its achievement—"material prosperity, wealth, produce, laborsaving machines, iron, cotton, . . . railways, intercommunication and trade with lands, steamships, mining, general employment, . . . cheap appliances for comfort, numberless technical schools, books, newspapers." What remains to be achieved is "a sublime and serious Religious Democracy,"[18] "the moral civilization" denoted by "right, justice, truth."

When Walt Whitman wrote *Democratic Vistas*, the population of the United States was forty million. He foresaw the great expansion and growth in both area and population, and he gasped in amazement. "What an age! What a land!" he cried out. "Where, elsewhere, one so great?"[19] The "work of the New World is not ended," he wrote, "but only fairly begun."[20]

It is remarkable that *Democratic Vistas* is as current and relevant for the American Bicentennial as it was for the Centennial celebration. Our problems seem greater and more complex, but this may be a function of the different order of magnitude. In essential human terms it is as though Walt Whitman had written his tract for our time no less than for his own.

And no less remarkable is the way in which *Democratic Vistas* expresses the essence of the Hebraic spirit and tries to define the "American idea" or the American program. Yet there is no denigration of the material, physical aspects of man's life on earth; there is no elevation of poverty to a high value. Time and again the Hebrew Scriptures command care of the poor, who are seen as belonging to the same class of suffering humanity as the stranger, the widow, the orphan. What sane person would seek to become a widow or an orphan—or a poor man? As Samuel Johnson observed: "All the arguments which are brought to represent poverty as no evil show it to be a great evil. You never find people laboring to convince you that you may live very happily with a plentiful fortune."[21] To live only on the level of sheer necessity is to live on the level of sheer animality

—a level that falls far short of that attainable by humanity. In choosing a life of plenty—based on intelligence, invention, industry, cooperation—America seeks to identify itself with life and the blessing as these were seen in the Hebrew Scriptures:

Blessed shall you be in the city, and blessed shall you be in the field. Blessed shall be the fruit of your body, and the fruit of your ground, and the fruit of your beasts, the increase of your cattle, and the young of your flock. Blessed shall be your basket and your kneading-trough. . . .[22] The Lord God will make you abundantly prosperous in all the work of your hand, in the fruit of your body, and in the fruit of your cattle, and in the fruit of your ground.[23]

But this is only one-half of the American-Hebraic idea. The other half is what Emerson referred to as "the law of love and justice"; what Theodore Parker had in mind when he spoke of the idea of inalienable rights, the idea that all men are created equal, of a democratic government based on "the principles of eternal justice, the unchanging law of God"; what Walt Whitman pointed to when he spoke of "right, justice, truth," of America's "moral civilization," of "absolute Conscience, moral soundness, Justice," "a sublime and serious Religious Democracy." These conceptions all point to the claim that America, like Israel, is an exception among nations. Adapting the words of Buber: America may not make its own existence the absolute for which it exists. The absolute for which it exists is *something transcendent and faces it.* National power and national well-being, of great importance as supporters of and contributors to the good life, are not the ultimate values that the nation may revere.

The dependence of national well-being on the moral quality of the nation is one of the main themes of the Hebrew Scriptures and perhaps its most characteristic note. God sent Jeremiah to say to the King of Judah: "Thus says the Lord: Do justice and righteousness and deliver from the hand of the oppressor him who has been robbed. And do no wrong or violence to the alien, the fatherless, and the widow, nor shed innocent blood in this place. . . . But if you will not heed these words, I swear by myself, says the Lord, that this house shall become a desolation."[24] The blessing is always conditional. "All the commandments which I command you this day you shall be careful to do, that you may live. . . . Man does not live by bread alone but . . . by everything that proceeds out of the mouth of the Lord."[25]

J. L. Tamon has pointed out that the State of Israel has emerged "as one of the few countries in the contemporary jaded world with a sense of purpose."[26] This was true of the Jewish nation from its very beginning; and the same judgment, by and large, may be made of the United States.

And the world, fairly or unfairly, seems to assume that this is the case and accordingly makes much greater demands of Israel and of the United States than it does of other countries or nations. In *To Jerusalem and Back*, Saul Bellow, with a note of bitterness, has said:

While Israel fought for life, debaters weighed her sins and especially the problem of the Palestinians. In this disorderly century refugees have fled from many countries. In India, in Africa, in Europe, millions of human beings have been put to flight, transported, enslaved, stampeded over the borders, left to starve, but only the case of the Palestinians is held permanently open. Where Israel is concerned, the world swells with moral consciousness. Moral judgment, a wraith in Europe, becomes a full-blooded giant when Israel and the Palestinians are mentioned.[27]

Bellow quotes Sartre as saying, "We demand more from this state," and Talmon as noting that the right of Israel to exist has to be won by special exertions, "by some special atonement, through being better than others," and Bellow observes that while European radicals have put aside their moral expectations and prefer to predict that history, itself a moral engine, will produce just societies through revolution or the class struggle, they do have moral expectations from the Jews—they believe "that the Jews, with their precious and refining record of suffering, have a unique obligation to hold up the moral burdens everyone else has dumped."[28]

Anti-Semitism may be offered as an explanation or cause of this phenomenon; but then this only substitutes one mystery for another, for a whole series of questions can be asked, Why the anti-Semitism?[29] We can only guess and argue over the causes, while the phenomenon itself can hardly be questioned.

A historian writing about Rush Welter's *The Mind of America, 1820–1860*, has noted: "The title is *The Mind of America*. Some years ago Henry Steele Commager wrote *The American Mind*; Perry Miller wrote of *The Life of the Mind in America*; and W. J. Cash wrote *The Mind of the South*. Is this assumption that one can generalize about the 'mind' of a society peculiar to Americans? We do not have books on the English Mind, the Scottish Mind, and still less on the British Mind." The author went on to say that most recent works in Britain assume that there can be no such thing as a single "mind," and that this is equally true of the work of European historians, who stress differences of class, culture, and tradition "at the expense of underlying national characteristics." "The fact that intelligent American scholars, who have immersed themselves in the sources, believe that it is possible to do this for their country says something interesting and important about American civilization; or at least about its history as interpreted by earlier generations and still accepted implicitly even by radical historians."[30]

The "underlying national characteristics" that constitute the "American mind" or the "American idea" were stated clearly in the Report of the President's Commission on National Goals (the appointment of the Commission by President Dwight D. Eisenhower and its very name are themselves characteristically and uniquely American):

The paramount goal of the United States was set long ago. It is to guard the rights of the individual, to ensure his development, and to enlarge his opportunity. It is set forth in the Declaration of Independence. . . . The goals we here identify are within the framework of the original plan and are calculated to bring to fruition the dreams of the men who laid the foundation of this country.

They stated their convictions quite simply: "We hold these truths

to be self-evident, that all men are created equal, that they are endowed by their Creator with certain unalienable Rights, that among
these are Life, Liberty, and the pursuit of Happiness. That to secure
these rights, Governments are instituted among Men, deriving their
just powers from the consent of the governed."

It was a mighty vision. . . . It inspires us still.[31]

III

In the last years of the American Revolution, Crève-
cœur, a Frenchman who traveled in America, posed the question, "What then is the American, this new man?" In a perceptive, thoughtful essay he wrote in the early 1940's, the late
Arthur M. Schlesinger, Sr., attempted to answer this question.[32]
This "new man" manifested certain traits that had become
characteristic of him.

"First and foremost is the habit of work." Schlesinger quoted
an American woman who countered an observation made by a
European that our difficulty was that we had no leisure class.
"But we have them," she replied, "only we call them tramps."
The European's comment then was: "America is the only coun-
try in the world where one is ashamed of having nothing to do."

Second, Americans became mechanically inventive—a race
of whittlers and tinkers, "daily engaged in devising, improving
and repairing tools and other utensils until, as Emerson said,
they had 'the power and habit of invention in their brain.'"

Third, Americans accepted versatility as an outstanding
attribute. In public affairs, Schlesinger believed with President
Andrew Jackson that any intelligent person could discharge the
duties of any public office—one did not need to be born to rule;
and in the common pursuits of life one could move freely from
job to job, "in marked contrast to the European custom of following occupations which often descended from father to son."

Fourth, Americans were extravagant and wasteful in the
use—or misuse and abuse—of their resources. They wore out

the land, destroyed forests, and easily moved on to virgin tracts. It was not until the opening years of the twentieth century that America adopted a national policy of conservation of natural resources. But by the time this occurred, Americans had already a tradition of wasteful living.

Fifth, Americans were mobile people. Both rural and urban dwellers moved, almost habitually, from place to place. But even more important than geographical or horizontal mobility was the social or vertical movement. Anybody might easily become somebody. Accordingly, there arose the "ingrained belief in equality of opportunity, the right of all men to a free and fair start." This led to the establishment of free tax-supported schools. But this "was far from being a dogma of enforced equality. To benefit from equality of opportunity a man must be equal to his opportunities. . . . The upshot was a conception of democracy rigorously qualified by individualism."

Sixth, this individualism at times assumed forms that defied government. Men countered government with the claim that they enjoyed "unalienable Rights." Sometimes these claims were pushed to the point of becoming lynch law, mob action, civil war, defiance of the Fugitive Slave Act, states' rights and nullification, and other checks on the abuse of governmental powers as a safeguard of minority rights.

Seventh, an important aspect of individualism was the cultivation of the acquisitive spirit. Having "equality of opportunity with plenty for all," Americans eagerly struggled to climb out of one class into a higher one.

But in contrast to Europe, America had practically no misers. Wealth was not loved for its own sake. Wealth "was the means of living a life of human dignity. It was a symbol of idealism rather than materialism." The American who was "this new man" freely shared his wealth with the less fortunate; he endowed charities, schools, hospitals, art galleries, and nourished "humanitarian undertakings which might otherwise have died a-borning."

Eighth, another national attitude was optimism. It was the quality essential to those coming here to seek and make for themselves a new home and a new life. To doubt the future was to invite disaster. Americans believed that for every evil there must be a remedy, and they saw no reason why they should not seek it or why they should not find it. This trait may have led to some unseemly boastfulness, for Americans tended to glorify the future even as Europeans tended to glorify the past.

This is the substance of Schlesinger's answer to Crève-cœur's question, "What then is the American, this new man?" But in the early 1940's Schlesinger saw that, as rural life was giving way to urbanization, certain modifications would be inevitable. Though most of the traits continued to thrive in the new situation, a few disappeared, and some were moderated.

One change was the importance that came to be attached to cultural achievement. City life released intellectual and artistic powers for which there was no room, no stimulation, in rural settings. The city had the best colleges and schools, the best newspapers and magazines; it had the bookstores, the libraries, the publishing houses, concert halls, art museums, theaters. There the artists or writers had contact with Europeans; there they found audiences and financial support; and Americans began to make contributions to science, scholarship, literature, and the fine arts that challenged comparison with the best that Europeans could offer.

A second change was that the earlier aversion to specialization of talent vanished. As life became more complex, a higher value was placed on the mastering of special skills or talents in industry, trade, the arts, and the sciences.

A third change was the great impetus given to voluntary associative activity. The rural environment nurtured liberty and equality; the city added "the boon of fraternity." Reformers, businessmen, workers, sportsmen—these and others—gravitated into special groups to further their special interests. Group or associative activity "came to be a sovereign principle of life."

A fourth change was the discrediting of individualism "as the automatic cure of social and economic ills." Farmers demanded government intercession to protect their right to make a living, and the average man began to believe that changed conditions had imposed the duty on government to safeguard the opportunities of all the people. This was a conviction without an ideology or doctrine; it was "the product of an adjustment to new times for the sake of preserving the traditional spirit of self-reliance and free competition." The work ethic particularly was affected by the changes; for at first it was believed that all men should work; then this became transformed into a doctrine of the right to work—a right claimed when and as opportunities for work lessened; and then the right to work became the duty of society to provide the opportunities.

Summarizing these developments, Schlesinger fairly commented that probably not one of the traits was peculiarly American, yet the aggregate "represents a way of life unlike that of any other nation."

The American is still "this new man"; there is still something that may be spoken of, however loosely, as the American mind or the American idea.

IV

But a whole generation has passed since Schlesinger wrote his perceptive and judicious summary of the American character as it had been and as it had become. Since then we have seen some startling changes.

Perhaps the most significant change has been a further denigration and weakening of the work ethic. There is no longer the traditional stress on thrift, the firm expectation of upward mobility, and the virtue of self-reliance—the idea of individuals making their own world, by their own hard work and qualities of body and mind. Although Americans take pride in maintaining a system of private entrepreneurship or enterprise, in fact we look to the governmental and social orders for a no-risk life —a system that will guarantee income for the farmer, the businessman, the worker, the unemployed, the sick, the aged, the poor, the young. In place of thrift, the emphasis is placed on borrowing, on credit; banks represent themselves mainly as lending institutions. The no-risk ethic looks to society's agencies to build vast housing complexes, to support massive universities at which almost anyone may attend, and to offer security against almost any and every risk—including the risk of a marriage or a pregnancy no longer desired.

The most radical change may prove to be the erosion of the work ethic. With a large percentage of young people, especially among blacks and other racial and ethnic minorities, unable to find employment, the psychological and moral values of work tend to become identified with a discredited bourgeois culture. After the passage of a little time, the unemployed young person is inclined to ask, "Who wants to work anyway? What's the big deal about working?" The real test of the durability of the work ethic can come only when there is "full employment" or when jobs go looking for workers; but where is the optimist who expects to see such a situation? What is much more likely is a continuation of established policies: Congress making appropriations for public works projects, for public service jobs in state and local governments, for youth training and job programs, for a Young Adult Conservation Corps, and similar makeshift aids and remedies for an ailing economy.

But it is not only the seven or eight millions of unemployed who question or challenge the traditional virtues of the work ethic. After all, we must bear in mind that over ninety million Americans were employed in 1977, and that in that year alone, some four million new jobs opened up. The American economy may be ailing, but it is far from being deathly sick and continues to be the cornerstone of the world economy. What appears to have happened—or to be happening before our eyes—is that, generally, even for millions of employed men and women, work seems to have lost its ethical force or quality. People no longer tend to think of or define themselves in terms of the work that occupies most of their days and years. In their eyes, their work is no longer undeniably rewarding. Each person can easily be replaced by another or by a machine or a new twist in technology.

The distance that has set in between people and their work generates a distance between themselves and society, between themselves and their fellows, and between themselves and the moral order. They no longer feel responsible for themselves and their fate; everything wrong can be blamed on the "system." If one does not relish one's job, it is because of the greed or callousness of the corporation, or the corruption of the union, or because "Washington" fails to provide ample support for domestic industry against foreign competition or the drought, or because of "Wall Street" and its evil influences on banks, the Federal Reserve System, and Congress. The "alienation" becomes general; one can see oneself easily divorced from one's spouse and separated from one's children; one can readily move from the East to the West or from the North to the South, or from the city to the suburbs or to a rural area. If there is a new interest in "roots," it is in genealogy, in family pedigrees; it does not necessarily mean an intensified closeness to one's own immediate family, for all indications are that the family is a weakened institution. On the contrary, Americans seem to have become destitute of roots—to be living with roots very near the surface, so that they can be transplanted readily into other jobs, other homes, other cities or towns, other families.

V

Thus we see that some of our most traditional, most basic ideas and institutions are threatened and face an uncertain future. There is indisputably a great uneasiness and apprehensiveness; the hold on the "American idea" is by no means as strong in the time of the American Bicentennial as it was when Walt Whitman wrote his *Democratic Vistas*. It is easy to find justification for saying today that Americans find it difficult, if not impossible, to feel a sense of national purpose.

And yet, having said all this, I hasten to add that there is no sense of despair. There is uncertainty, uneasiness, a sense of apprehensiveness, but there is no folding of the hands and waiting to be overtaken by fate and death. While some have turned to Eastern philosophies or religions of escape and withdrawal, and others are involved in unusual life-styles and systems of values, such interests are not likely to endure or to leave a permanent mark on many persons. On the whole, I believe that Americans remain Hebraic-Biblical in their spiritual culture, and heirs of Greece and Rome, of the Renaissance, the Reformation, and the Enlightenment. We continue to seek ways and means to fulfill the promise of life, liberty, and the pursuit of happiness. Perhaps more than any other people, we continue to argue for and to vindicate the belief in "self-evident" truths and in "certain unalienable Rights." The underlying principles on which our institutions of government were founded remain largely unchanged; we expect the leaders of our government to conduct their public lives on sound principles.

The Americans of 1776 were human beings, not angels. Their grievances against King George were not all of a high spiritual order. Among the "oppressions" enumerated by the Declaration of Independence were such mundane ones as that "He has erected a multitude of New Offices, and sent hither swarms of Officers to harass our People, and eat out their substance. . . . [He is responsible for] cutting off our Trade with all parts of the world. For imposing taxes on us without our Consent." American idealism was never wholly divorced from worldly considerations.

But neither are our worldly considerations today altogether free of idealistic elements. There is still an ideal America. There is still an America that is deeply concerned with inequalities of opportunity; an America that wants to wage war on poverty, to remove it root and branch; that seeks equal dignity and opportunity for women; that desperately seeks to find ways to become color-blind; that wants to right some wrongs done to American Indians; that tries to protect inmates of its prisons in their claims for constitutional rights, even including freedom of speech and press; that throws the protection of the Bill of Rights over its aliens no less than over its citizens; that tries to wipe out old legal obstacles imposed on children born out of wedlock; that tries to include public school pupils among the people entitled to the benefits of the First Amendment and of the Due Process Clause of the Fourteenth Amendment; that tries to keep church and state separate and totally independent, and to fulfill, in the greatest measure possible, the guarantee of religious liberty; that is constantly concerned with improvements in its administration of justice, and in protecting the person charged with crime no less than in protecting the interests of society; that firmly believes in and clings to the Rule of Law; that believes that human rights should be the concern of human beings wherever human beings are found.

There is still, therefore, the "American idea"—the "idea" that was the concern of Theodore Parker, of Ralph Waldo Emerson, and of Walt Whitman; and it is to this idea, with its Biblical, Judaic roots and analogues, to which this book is addressed. There is no claim that we are gods, but as Matthew Arnold wrote in a copy of Emerson's *Essays*, we can say properly enough that "the seeds of godlike power are in us still." There are ever more days to dawn. This more than suffices for human dignity, a sense of dedication, and the precious gift of hope for a future unknown and for things unseen.

1 /

Human Dignity:

From Creation to Constitution

THE SCENE IS FAMILIAR: Socrates is in prison under sentence of death; Crito comes to him with the news that Socrates does not really need to die the next day, for his friends can bribe the jailkeepers so that he may escape and be taken to Thessaly, where Crito's friends will look after the old man; but Socrates refuses to accept this little scheme and proceeds to explain why. His fellow Athenians, he says, have done an evil thing by handing down an unjust verdict against him, but a good man will not return evil for evil. But why would it be evil for him to escape? Well, Socrates argues, he would be breaking not only the unjust law made in his case by Athens, but the total legal order; and then he proceeds to paint a touching, sentimental picture of what that legal order had done for him. By its terms, his father and mother became legally husband and wife; and when he was born, it was the legal order that made him their son. And it was by reason of the compulsory education laws that he was trained in literature, music, dancing, and gymnastics. He was, therefore, the child and servant of these laws, which are to him like a father and a master. "Would you," Socrates asked on behalf of the laws, "have any right to strike or abuse or do any other harm to your father or your master, if you had one, because you had been struck or abused by him?" Then Socrates says that the laws and government of Athens spoke to him in these terms:

Has a philosopher like you failed to discover that our country is more to be valued and higher and holier far than mother or father or any ancestor, and more to be regarded in the eyes of the gods and of men of understanding? to be reverenced and humoured in its anger, even more than a father, and either to be persuaded, or if not persuaded, to be obeyed? And when we are punished by her, whether with imprisonment or stripes, the punishment is to be endured in silence; and if she leads us to wounds or death in battle, we must comply; that is our duty: a man may not yield or retreat or leave his rank, but whether in battle or in a court of law, or in any other place, he must do what his city and his country order him; or he must change their view of what is just: and if he may do no violence to his father or mother, much less may he do violence to his country.[1]

What a far cry is this paean to the state from the substance and tone of John Locke's *Second Treatise of Civil Government* and *A Letter Concerning Toleration*; for Locke takes as his fundamental premise the proposition that Adam, the paradigmatic man, was the child of God and not of the state. Indeed, it is men who make the state rather than the state that makes men. Men in the state of nature, he says, have children, and the *parents* have the duty to take care of them "during the imperfect state of childhood." This duty includes the education of the child's mind "till reason shall take its place and ease them of that trouble."[2] It is the *parents, and not the state*, that have the power to form the character of their children by bringing them up in a culture and religion of their choice.[3]

The fifth of the Ten Commandments is to honor one's father and mother. According to the rabbis of the Talmud, there are three partners in the creation of each person: God, the father, and the mother. There is no commandment in the Bible to honor one's state, nor is there a teaching that the state is a partner with the parents in the formation of the child. But Socrates, and the Greeks generally, would have had a commandment to honor one's state as if it were one's father and mother. If Plato had written Genesis, he would have had God create the state on the sixth day, and only subsequently would have appeared Adam.

Socrates felt overawed when, on the day of his death, he thought of all that he owed Athens; Locke could stand at a distance from the state and take its measure against Adam, the creature of God, a creature that could live a fairly decent, good life *without* the state, though a better, richer, and more secure life as a citizen—provided, of course, that he is a citizen of a state that respects the individual as a creature of God and not as a creature of the state. 2082084

But if we were to stop here in our contrast between Socrates and Locke, we would be unjust to Socrates, who invented or discovered the soul, that thing to which one must be true even at the cost of one's life. But this belief in the soul was on its own track, separate and apart from the political track. At no point did it seem to influence the political theory of Socrates. His belief in the soul, and the duty he felt to awaken his fellow citizens to the fact that they, too, had souls that come from and will return to God, affected deeply the course of Western thought and the course of his life—a course that brought him into conflict with his city-state; yet the belief did not lead him into a political theory that could be molded to accommodate the human soul and the demands that souls may make. The Socratic political theory remained earthbound, and in its essentials was undifferentiated from the conventional Hellenic views, beliefs, and loyalties.

But Locke, who had inherited the Socratic belief in the soul, and the many deposits to that belief made by centuries of religious and cultural history, was able to build that belief into the very structure of his political theory because his building blocks were Biblical and not Greek—essentially Biblical though admittedly weathered by the forces of many centuries of religious, intellectual, political, and economic history.

The contrast between Socrates and Locke as to the duty of educating the young and what that duty implies for political obligation and theory can be brought out if we consider the exit visa fees imposed by the U.S.S.R. on Jews who wished to leave for settlement in Israel. The government demanded that the applicant for such a visa reimburse the state for the cost of the applicant's education, a fee that might be equivalent to ten to twelve years' salary. One cannot help thinking of Socrates and his moving statement of gratitude to Athens as his educator. But paying the state for one's education makes good sense, even when reduced to mere bookkeeping terms, only if one sees the individual as solely and exclusively the creature of the state—then, and then only, is it true that all that one is and has one owes to the state. If the state has taught one to be a dentist, an engineer, or a violinist, then the state can compel that person to work at his calling, and if he decides to give up his Soviet (or Athenian) citizenship, he is a debtor and the state may force him to repay what he owes. The logic is clear *if the individual is absorbed by the citizen*.

But if we think of students as children who owe their lives to God, and of parents as the ones who have the primary duty of educating them, then schools and school laws, *and the state itself*, become mere means to ends that may transcend the state. If the child receives free schooling, it is because the parents—all parents—have pooled their resources, through taxes, to build and maintain a system of common schools, from kindergarten through professional schools. It is still the *parents* who fulfill their duties to their children; it is still the *parents* who pay for the education; it is still the *parents* who help their children choose and direct their course of preparation for life and their work. From this point of view, it is tyrannical for a state to demand reimbursement from those who feel that they made a grave mistake when they studied dentistry or engineering. After all, their investment was more than something on which a price tag could be placed—they were losing years of their lives. In a free society—one based on Lockean premises—no point would be made in such instances; no government would dare to pour salt on the open wound.

In this context the letter and spirit of the decision and opinion of the United States Supreme Court in *Pierce* v. *Society of Sisters of the Holy Name* is illuminating. The state of Oregon in 1925 enacted a statute that prohibited parochial and private schools for children between eight and sixteen years of age. Children could attend only public schools. The Supreme Court unanimously held the statute invalid. Children, said the Court, are not mere creatures of the state. "The fundamental theory of liberty upon which all governments in this Union repose," said the Court, "excludes any general power of the state to standardize its children by forcing them to accept instruction from public teachers only. The child is not the mere creature of the state; those who nurture him and direct his destiny have the right, coupled with the high duty, to recognize and prepare him for additional obligations."[4] So, too, in 1972, when Wisconsin tried to compel Amish children to attend secondary school up to the age of sixteen, against the religious beliefs of the parents, the Supreme Court held that such compulsion contravened the rights of the parents under the Free Exercise Clause of the First Amendment.[5]

These decisions are fruits of the Lockean tree. They are consequences of a political theory that is founded on Biblical conceptions of our nature and of the world in which we are born, live, and die.

II

The starting point for Locke, as it is for any theorist of human rights, is the belief *that we are more than citizens*. It is not merely that we *have* souls. It is that we *are* souls—divinely created beings, invested with rights and dignities at birth, subject to God-made laws and ordinances, and responsible to our Maker. We cannot divest ourselves of this God-given nature. The time may come for us to become citizens of Athens or Rome or Jerusalem, but our citizenship will not be all-absorbing. We will always retain certain rights and liberties, certain powers and dignities—prerogatives that we enjoy as gifts from the Giver of gifts, and which we can never lose.

The idea that certain essential rights and liberties are inseparable from the very conception of human existence has its deepest and most productive roots in many Biblical conceptions, as we will see, including the idea of covenant, the idea of man made in the image of God, the belief that every man or woman is free to choose between good and evil, and the idea that the right law is ultimately founded on the righteousness of God and not on the will of any human being, even if he be king or judge.

But other streams of thought have also made contributions to the development of the theory of human rights: the teachings of the Stoic philosophers regarding the inviolability of human dignity; the natural law philosophy that has had a continuous life from the time of the late Roman Empire, through Thomas Aquinas and Richard Hooker, to the present time; the teachings of the Roman lawyers concerning a common law of nations or peoples, the *jus gentium*; the international law principles of Hugo Grotius and Samuel von Pufendorf; the writings of the French Enlightenment; the emphasis on the right of the individual conscience associated with the Protestant and Puritan reformations; the stress on the inherent dignity of man that can be found in the great Renaissance writers like Erasmus and Pico della Mirandola.

These ideas and beliefs, joined with certain wars and revolutions—from the conquests of Alexander the Great through the American and French revolutions—and with international involvements of peoples, religions, cultures, and goods, culminated in the Bill of Rights of the United States Constitution, the French Declaration of the Rights of Man and of the Citizen, and over a century and a half later, in the United Nations Declaration of Human Rights.

All these developments—all these conceptions, ideas, documents—take as their underlying foundation the distinction between man and citizen—not the Socratic distinction between *body and soul*, but the Biblical, and later Lockean, distinction between *man and citizen*.

Thus, the basic French document is expressly denominated as the Declaration of the Rights of *Man* and of the *Citizen*. These categories, while they are bound to overlap, since every citizen is also a man or a woman, are not to be confused. Some of the articles are concerned with the rights of man—Article 1, for example, states that "men are born and remain free and equal in respect of rights." Article 6, however, is concerned with the enactment of statutes, and so provides that "all citizens," personally or through representation, have a right to participate in the formation of positive law.

The Bill of Rights of the United States Constitution mentions only "people." It is people, and not only citizens, who have freedom of religion, freedom of speech and the press, freedom of assembly; security in their persons, houses, and papers against unreasonable searches and seizures; guarantees against excessive bail and against cruel and unusual punishments; and all the other enumerated guarantees. The Thirteenth Amendment against slavery and involuntary servitude is for the protection of all people, and the Due Process and Equal Protection Clauses of the Fourteenth Amendment are guarantees expressly made for the benefit of "any person."

The thirty Articles of the United Nations Declaration of Human Rights all speak in terms of "everyone," or "all human beings." Article 2 provides that "everyone is entitled to all the rights and freedoms set forth in this Declaration, without distinction of any kind, such as race, color, sex, language, religion, political or other opinion, national or social origin, property, birth or other status." It is hard to see how language could more clearly express the idea that the rights enumerated in the Declaration are to be enjoyed by "persons," by "all human beings," by "everyone," and not only by citizens.[6]

These documents share the common presupposition that since human rights are different from, though basic to, the rights of citizens, they are not dependent upon any constitution, upon the grant from any ruler or government. The fundamental human rights are provided for in the unwritten constitution of human nature—a constitution that is beyond the reach of any government or earthly power.

This was essentially the view of Thomas Jefferson and of the framers of the Constitution and its Bill of Rights. The Constitution was adopted though it had no Bill of Rights, because the latter was deemed to be unnecessary for a free society with a government that was to have only delegated powers.

Writing from Paris on December 20, 1787, Jefferson told James Madison that although their political theory made a Bill of Rights technically unnecessary, "a bill of rights is what the people are entitled to against every government on earth, . . . and what no just government should refuse," nor should its existence be permitted to "rest on inference."[7] The Bill of Rights as it was first submitted by Madison to Congress in 1789 contained the following provisions as the first article:

1. That all power is originally vested in, and consequently derived from, the people.

That government is instituted and ought to be exercised for the benefit of the people; which consists in the enjoyment of life and liberty, with the right of acquiring and using property, and generally of pursuing and obtaining happiness and safety.

That the people have an indubitable, unalienable, and indefeasible right to reform or change their government, whenever it be found adverse or inadequate to the purposes of its institution.

Nothing could state more clearly and definitively the basic, most essential concepts of the philosophy of human rights: (1) that people are prior to and always are more than citizens; (2) that people make states and governments; that states and governments are formed by people to serve their own interests and needs; that governments are formed to enhance people's enjoyment of their basic human rights; that no majority—no government—may deprive individuals of their fundamental human rights.

III

The Biblical story of Creation has a special significance, in our context, for establishing the idea that there is an eternal order that is prior to and independent of human life—an order that is both natural and moral, an order that is divinely ordained and unalterable.

For the same God who created the sun and the moon created Adam and Eve; and just as He was the law-maker for the former, so, too, was He the law-maker for the latter. If God can make the laws that regulate the physical bodies, He can also make the moral laws that should guide the actions of human beings. All these laws—both physical and moral—are part of the eternal order that was prior to and independent of Adam and Eve, Cain and Abel, and Noah and his sons and daughters. No man, no king or government, can alter that moral order, can repeal or amend the moral law. No king can make the killing of an innocent person anything other than *what it is*: murder. The act has a moral nature, and that is something no one can change. It is from this that we get the notion of a Higher Law— a kind of unwritten constitution for mankind, which no statute, ordinance, or judgment may contradict. From it we also get the notion of the Rule of Law—the idea that governance excludes arbitrariness, willfulness, unreasonableness, and that all things, events, and actions are subject to law.

It is this basic Biblical postulate—that the moral no less than the physical order of the universe is founded in Creation— that is the burden of the answer out of the whirlwind in Job. He who made the hippopotamus gave him his physical nature, so that he lies under the lotus plants and among the willows of the brook. So, too, the crocodile, whose back is made of rows of shields, whose sneezings flash forth light, and from whose mouth go flaming torches. Can Job understand the thoughts and plans of Him who is their maker? And if he does not understand the physical laws, yet knows that they are operative, why should he doubt the operation of the moral laws, of whose operations he is equally ignorant? A man who does not know the way to the dwelling of light, who has not entered the storehouses of the snow, who has not commanded the morning since his days began, such a man can be wise only in his own conceit—and yet he dares to question the ways of God with those who practice inequity and with those who follow the paths of justice! "Shall a faultfinder contend with the Almighty?" The righteous man may suffer, and he may see the evil flourish, yet he must not doubt the righteousness of God and deny God's justice and power. Though the Biblical man move in ignorance and darkness as to the ways of God and His moral laws, yet he remains, through all trials and afflictions, the man who trusts his Creator—"that a godless man shall not come before Him." [8] He trusts God that the sun will rise and set, and that fire will burn and snow will freeze. "I shall never believe," said Einstein, "that God plays dice [or games] with the world. . . . The Lord God is subtle, but malicious He is not." The Biblical man of faith believed that God does not play moral tricks; that in the moral realm He is as subtle as in the physical realm, and that in neither realm is He malicious.

What it all comes to is the belief that we are born into a world for which there are preordained moral, no less than physical, laws—moral laws which we may not break with impunity.

"Though the mills of God grind slowly, yet they grind exceeding small." And no one, not even the most exalted and powerful king, can change these laws, these ways of God, by a jot or a tittle. One can therefore never be totally and exclusively a citizen. One can never be subject only to the laws of one's state. One is first and always a human being, created by God, and a citizen of a world of which God is King and law-maker. In God's domain, where His law prevails, every individual has the dignity that comes from being God's handiwork; all are equal because they are equally citizens of His city; they are all free because they are all, king and commoner alike, equally subject to the ordered liberty which He has ordained from the beginning of time and for all time.

IV

From the standpoint of Judaism, human rights—just as the Bible itself—must begin with Genesis, with God the Creator. For Judaism, human rights have their "beginning"—their *bereshet*—their foundation, outside the state, outside any man-made constitution or bill of rights, outside even humanity itself. Their beginning is linked with the beginning of the sun and moon, land and water, day and night, justice and law, good and evil, the blessing and the curse. Their beginning, their nature, their power, their truth, and their justice are in the power, righteousness, and holiness of God the Creator.

There is recorded in the Jerusalem Talmud a disputation between Rabbi Akiba and Ben Azzai as to which is the most fundamental principle of the Torah (the body of Jewish law or teaching). Akiba, quoting Leviticus, said: "Thou shalt love thy neighbor as thyself." Ben Azzai, quoting Genesis, "This is the book of the generations of Adam," said that this expressed a still greater principle.[9]

This exchange between two of the most famous ancient rabbis is reminiscent of the incident recorded of Jesus when he was asked which was the greater commandment in the law, and he answered, combining passages from Deuteronomy and Leviticus: "You shall love the Lord your God with all your heart, and with all your soul, and with all your mind," and "You shall love your neighbor as yourself." Jesus concluded by saying: "On these two commandments depend all the law and the prophets." [10]

It should be noted that Akiba and Ben Azzai were not discussing what they thought was the greatest commandment but rather the greatest principle (*klal godol*), while Jesus was asked to state what he believed to be the greatest commandment. While the answer of Akiba was a commandment as well as a principle, that of Ben Azzai was only a principle, namely, the doctrine that all men are descended from the one and same ancestor, that all men share a common origin and a common, identical dignity. The full passage cited by Ben Azzai reads as follows: "This is the book of the generations of Adam [man]. When God created man [Adam] He made him in the likeness of God." [11]

Ben Azzai's answer is by far the more convincing one, for without it the love commandment has no metaphysical base; it stands as a naked assertion of God's will, in no way different from many other commandments. But the text chosen by Ben Azzai goes to the very nature of man, for it says that all men are the children of one father; that just as their father—Adam—was made in the image of God, so each man, a son of Adam, is made in God's image; that there is only one human family; that all human beings are born with equal dignity; that all human beings are equal. It is on the basis of this principle—this *klal godol*—that God, the maker of Adam, can say to the children of Adam: "Love thy neighbor as thyself."

With the dispute between Akiba and Ben Azzai before him, Hermann Cohen said that the latter was evidently right; for the love of the neighbor is "dependent upon God's creation of man, and not upon the subjective feeling with which I love myself or somebody else. 'This is the book of the generation of man . . . in the likeness of God made He him.' Upon this principle rests the history of mankind."[12]

One might say that Jewish thought and ethics are almost constantly driven back to their sources in God the Creator. In one example of this way of thinking and feeling, when a Jewish court had jurisdiction in capital cases the law required that the judges charge the witnesses against the accused in the following terms:

Perhaps what you are about to say is mere conjecture or hearsay, based on secondhand information, on what you heard from a trustworthy person. Perhaps you are unaware that we will in the course of the trial subject you to inquiry and query. Know that capital cases are unlike monetary cases. In a monetary case, one may make restitution and his offense is expiated; but in a capital case (the witness) is accountable for the blood of the man and the blood of his (potential) posterity until the end of time. Thus with respect to Cain it is said: "The voice of thy brother's bloods crieth" (Gen. 4:10)—that is, his blood and the blood of his (potential) descendants. For this reason, but a single man was created, to teach us that if any man destroys a single life in the world, Scripture imputes it to him as though he had destroyed the whole world; and if any man preserves one life, Scripture ascribes it to him as though he had preserved the whole world. Furthermore, all human beings are fashioned after the pattern of the first man, yet no two faces are exactly alike. Therefore, every man may well say, "For my sake the world was created." And perhaps you will say, "Why borrow this trouble?" It is said: "He being a witness, whether he hath seen or known, if he do not utter it, then he shall bear his iniquity" (Lev. 5:1). And perhaps you will say, "Why should we incur guilt for the blood of this man?" It is written: "And when the wicked perish, there is joy" (Prov. 11:10).[13]

One of the characteristic aspects of Judaism is marked dramatically in the above passage, that is, the inextricable intermixture of metaphysical, ethical, and legalistic strands—the way normative thought allows itself to be bitten into by meta-

physical principles. Here stands before the court an ordinary
man who, in a preliminary inquiry, had qualified to testify as a
witness in a case in which another ordinary man is on trial for
his life, and the witness and the accused are suddenly transported to the time and place of the very creation of man. The
witness is made to feel that it is no ordinary creature who faces
life or death, but Adam himself, and the whole of mankind, and
the whole of creation, which was made for Adam, who can
enjoy creation only as long as he has life. Yet it was not, of
course, the judges who cast this terrifying, awesome burden on
the witness—they merely reminded him of what God the Creator had done when He fashioned man on the sixth day after all
His other work had been accomplished, and fashioned him in
His own image.

V

In the second century, in order to establish the abso-
luteness, newness, and uniqueness of the Christian religion,
Marcion contended that there were two Gods: the God of the
Hebrew Scriptures, who was the Creator and Judge; and the
God of the Pauline Epistles, who was the God of love whom
Jesus had revealed. The God whom Judaism proclaimed was
the inferior God. He was the one who had made the material
universe, including man, and He ruled by law and justice. He
was the Ruler of the world of matter and bodies; He issued
commandments, and judged by works. The Christian God,
however, He whom Paul had proclaimed, was the God of pure
love, the God of spirit, the God of faith and grace. He had nothing to do with the world of nature but only with the world of
spirit; He did not judge, and He delivered only souls. He was
not the Messiah of the Hebrew Scriptures, and He could not
be expected to rescue man from the material world.

In Marcion we can see the Platonic dualism of matter and

spirit, the dualism of body and soul which Socrates had taught some four centuries before, a teaching which came to pervade much of Hellenistic thought and religion.

The Christian ecclesiastical leaders who became aware of Marcion's influence repudiated him and condemned Marcionism as a heresy. They put him on a level with the Gnostics, whom they severely condemned. For without the Hebrew Scriptures, they would have no Old Testament, and therefore there would be no new Israel, and there could be no claim that the promises of the Old Testament were meant for the new children of Israel. But the promises had to be fulfilled if the New Covenant was a true revelation. And how could there be monotheism if there were two Gods? And how could it be said that the Christian God had lacked the power to create the world? And if the Hebrew Scriptures spoke of a Messiah who was to come, was the God of Judaism, then, to produce him in the latter end of days? Marcionism had to be repudiated and condemned as heretical and as a thoroughly evil, heathenish teaching.

Though condemned, Marcion's teachings affected the bias and tone of Christianity, for though Christianity does not countenance the idea of two Gods, yet it always finds ways to belittle the God of whom Judaism has been the witness. He is the God of the material world, the God of Justice, the God of law, the God of rewards and punishment, the God of the past, while the Gospel proclaims the God of pure spirit, of pure love, of pure grace, of pure faith, the God of the future. The dualism of body and soul has remained basic in Christianity, and Pauline antinomianism has remained firmly rooted in the Christian religious consciousness.

But if there is truly—not merely rhetorically—a Judeo-Christian tradition of natural rights and human rights, it must be based on a metaphysics that recognizes the hand of God in matter and body, and in human nature and human beings; a metaphysics that sees the possibility of a reconciliation of law and justice with grace and love; and that hopes for the concord of nature and spirit. But above and underlying all, it must be based on the belief that the goodness and wisdom of God the Creator are somehow reflected in Adam whom He fashioned out of the dust of the earth. Only man having this transcendent dignity can be said to have "natural, imprescriptible, and inalienable rights."[14]

The Jewish contrast with Marcion is typified by the teaching of the great Jewish classic, *Duties of the Heart*, written in the eleventh century by Bahya ibn Paquda. It is one's duty, Bahya taught, to study the evidence of divine wisdom. The first mark of such wisdom is the very composition of the world: the earth and its elements, the oceans, fire, the atmosphere, the "unchanging balance and measure" of nature, which today we call ecology. The second mark of wisdom is the human species, "a universe on a small scale that completes the ordered series of creation." Third is the wisdom apparent in the formation of the individual human being, his physical structure and mental faculties. Man, says Bahya, "resembles the large universe; he is like the universe fundamentally and in its original elements." Fourth, man is to seek an understanding of the wisdom of the Creator as it is manifested in other species of living creatures, from the least to the greatest. The fifth mark of wisdom is studied in plants and minerals. The sixth is the mark of wisdom found in the sciences and arts and crafts, which the Creator has provided for man to enable him to live as a human being and to contribute to his improvement. Only last comes the wisdom found in the Torah, the study of which marks off the Jew from other people.

For our purposes it is important to note that the universal elements of Judaism, which clings to the belief in God the Creator, come ahead of the particularistic, and that the bonds of humanity come ahead, in the metaphysical order of God's goodness and wisdom, of the special bond or covenant between God and Israel.

What Bahya in effect teaches—and this is the teaching of Judaism—is that if we only knew God as the Creator, if we only knew His wisdom and goodness, made manifest to us by the light of reason alone, even if there had been no election of Israel and no giving of the Torah at Sinai, we could say "Dayenu!"—that is, in "His wisdom and goodness are enough mercy and grace." It is in this spirit that the Jew gives thanks each morning for the work of creation. Typical of these blessings or prayers is the following from the morning service:

> Praised art Thou, O Lord our God, King of the universe.
> Thou orders the cycles of light and darkness;
> Thou ordains the order of all creation.
> Thou causest light to shine over the earth;
> Thy radiant mercy is upon its inhabitants.
> In Thy goodness the work of creation
> Is continually renewed day by day.
> How manifold are Thy works, O Lord!
> With wisdom Thou did fashion them all!
> The earth teems with Thy creations.

Rabbi Joshua ben Levi said, "When a man goes on the road, a troupe of angels proceed in front of him and proclaim: 'Make way for the image of the Holy One, blessed be He.'" [15] And wherever man goes, on whatever road, he has the "unalienable Rights" with which "all men . . . are endowed by their Creator." [16]

It is all summed up in the glorious Psalm 8, in which the work of the first days of creation is intimately and indissolubly bound with the work accomplished on the sixth day:

When I look at Thy heavens, the work of Thy fingers,
    the moon and the stars which Thou has established;
What is man that Thou art mindful of him,
    and the son of man that Thou dost care for him?
Yet Thou hast made him little less than divine,

and dost crown him with glory and honor.
Thou hast given him dominion over the works of Thy hands;
　Thou hast put all things under his feet, . . .
O Lord, our Lord,
　how majestic is Thy name in all the earth!

The Psalmist does not glorify only those who are bound in the covenant of Abraham. He sings of man, of Adam. It is man, generic man—not the Jewish man, not the white man, but just man, Adam, made, the rabbis taught, of the dust gathered from all parts of the earth, so that no one race might claim that for them alone was the world made; it is undifferentiated, unhyphenated man who was made little less than divine, crowned with glory and honor, and given dominion over all the other works of creation. It is only of man so created and thus endowed that one can say that he has, by virtue only of his birth as man, the fundamental human rights that define and shield his God-given human dignity.

　Writing in 1932, impliedly separating himself from the world of Psalm 8, Carl Becker wrote: "What is man that the electron should be mindful of him? Man is but a foundling in the cosmos, abandoned by the forces that created him. Unparented, unassisted and undirected by omniscient or benevolent authority, he must fend for himself, and with the aid of his own limited intelligence find his way about in an indifferent universe."[17] But this burlesque of the psalm shrouds the fact that the Bible does not purport to state a fact but an ideal; for surely the psalmist knew that not every man was indeed crowned with glory and honor. But every man had the capacity, the potentiality, from birth, to become a little less than divine, to be crowned by God with glory and honor, and to take dominion over the works of His hands, and to have all things under his feet.

　And so, too, is it with the Declaration of Independence; for Jefferson knew that in fact all men were not equal, that all men did not in fact enjoy inalienable rights. The Declaration was intended as a statement of ideals, as a promise to change facts so that they would approximate more closely the ideals projected as a guide and a program. The intent of the Declaration conforms with the intent of the Hebrew Scriptures, that is, to build the city of man so that it would be hardly distinguishable from the City of God—a city planned, measured, and built on a model that conforms with "the Laws of Nature and of Nature's God."[18]

2 /

The Rule of Law:

Torah and the Constitution

The Rule of Law

When we look at Judaism as a system of values or
ideals, perhaps its most striking feature or characteristic is its
emphasis on law. Judaism may be described as a law-centered
civilization. The largest part of its classical and traditional literature consists of legal writings.[1] Besides the Torah, there are the
Mishnah, the Babylonian and the Jerusalem Talmuds, the
countless commentaries, novellae, codes, *takanoth* (decrees),
digests, and other sources and records of law, comprised in
thousands of volumes, and there is a great responsa literature,
the judgments and decisions of rabbis and *dayyanim* (judges).
According to Menachim Elon, this case law consists of approximately 300,000 judgments and decisions.[2] This is a staggering
number, especially when one considers that these judgments
and decrees were handed down by the judges of a people who
were generally without political independence and without
political power. When the rabbis thought of the immensity of
the Talmud, in its comprehensive sense, they spoke of it as a
sea. Rabbi Yitschak Meir of Ger asked a young man if he had

53

studied the Torah. "Just a little," said the young man. "That," said the rabbi, "is all that anyone has learned of the Torah."

But this sea, when compared with the American legal order, becomes only a lake. For American civilization, from its very beginning—and in part because our founding fathers thought of themselves as Israelites who had left Egypt and had entered the Promised Land, where they might live under the laws of God and not under the laws of men[3]—took on the quality of a law-centered civilization. In recent years we have been repeatedly and stridently reminded that violence has played a prominent role in the American character and in American history, and the facts, discounting their polemical exaggeration, ought not to be denied.[4] But violence is only one part of the American story, and by far the less important part. More important is to see that the American system and civilization are law-centered, perhaps as no secular civilization ever before has been.

It would take too long and it would divert us from our objective if I were to try to prove this proposition with detailed arguments, but I will cite only a few facts, comparable to those we used in discussing Jewish law. At the turn of the century there were more than 500,000 reported cases in over 6,000 volumes of reports published from colonial times to 1897. By now the number of reported, printed judgments and opinions comes to about two million. Annually, about 40,000 new reported cases are added. By 1976 the Supreme Court opinions were reported in approximately 425 volumes, comprising over a quarter of a million printed pages. Besides published court decisions, there are about 150,000 federal and state statutes. When the New York State Legislature convened in January 1974, its members faced a mountain of over 6,000 bills to consider and act on. The *Congressional Record*, which records the daily proceedings of the United States Congress, consisted of over 36,000 printed, double-columned pages of proceedings for the 1975 session (the First Session of the 94th Congress); indeed, the Government Printing Office employs about 2,500 workers to produce each day's record in about thirteen hours. Then there are the countless thousands of decisions and orders of the federal and state administrative agencies; the *Federal Register*, for example, which publishes current federal administrative regulations, runs each year to about 30,000 pages. And the National Labor Relations Board by now has well over 200 large volumes of opinions and decisions, comprising a total of about 150,000 pages. The authorities that give accreditation to law schools today require a *minimum* of 60,000 volumes in the law school library.

No country in the world can match the American legal record or can show a comparable reliance on legislation and law to settle disputes, to fix and express national ideals and social values, and to resolve political, regional, and ideological differences.

Sooner or later almost every important social, political, or moral issue is ultimately set on its way for resolution by the United States Supreme Court. In the last few years we saw this happen with the problem of racial segregation, the problem of abortion, the problem of legislative malapportionment, the problem of capital punishment. Our legislatures, on the whole, were inept or paralyzed—they could not or would not act—and the country was confused and agitated. These and many similar problems, of equal or lesser significance, were resolved by the Supreme Court. Whether the decisions were right or wrong, the best or the worst, is not relevant. The point is that they were resolved, not by violence, not by mobs taking to the streets, but by the Rule of Law, by resort to constitutional litigation, our closest approximation, outside the physical sciences, to the institutional use of reason and objective evidence in the resolution of human and social disputes and conflict. To stress violence as if it were the predominant character of American history is to see the shadow but not the sunlight.

Writing in 1953, the late Edward S. Corwin estimated that the Supreme Court had probably decided well over 4,000 cases involving questions of constitutional interpretation, and wrote that it is probable that at least 50,000 pages of the United States Supreme Court Reports were devoted to constitutional law topics.[5] By now the number of cases and of pages far exceeds Corwin's informed estimates. In some of these cases, the Supreme Court exercised to the extreme its power of judicial review of congressional action, and in 99 cases held acts of Congress to be unconstitutional.[6] In addition, the Court has declared unconstitutional 848 state statutes and 96 municipal ordinances.

And yet despite this record of conflict between the Court and Congress, and between the Court and the states, and despite the divided reception accorded many of the Court's decisions on delicate, and often even explosive, issues, only three times in a period of almost two centuries have the American people amended the Constitution in order to overrule decisions of the Supreme Court: the Eleventh Amendment, ratified in 1794, which overruled the decision in *Chisholm* v. *Georgia* that involved the right to sue a state; the Fourteenth Amendment, ratified in 1868, which overruled the decision in the *Dred Scott* case of 1857; and the Sixteenth Amendment, ratified in 1913, that overruled the decision that Congress had no constitutional power to levy a tax on incomes.[7] After the decisions of the Supreme Court in 1962 and 1963 declaring Bible-reading and prayers in public schools unconstitutional,[8] no less than 147 resolutions were introduced in the House of Representatives calling for a constitutional amendment to overrule these decisions; the House Judiciary Committee held hearings for seven weeks, but the members could not agree and did not bring a bill before the House. The issue was brought to life again in 1971 on a petition to take the proposed amendment directly to the House, but the proposed amendment failed to receive the required two-thirds majority. The bill to amend the Constitution to overrule the Court decisions failed despite the fact that before

Bible-reading and prayers in public schools were declared un-constitutional 37 States and the District of Columbia either allowed or required religious exercises in their public schools; it was estimated that a majority of the nation's schools conducted Bible reading. And yet opponents of the Court's decisions have failed in their efforts to have Congress pass the so-called Dirksen Amendment.[9]

What does this record mean? One thing it means, I believe, is that when the chips are down there is a national consensus that is predisposed to accept the Constitution, and that the Constitution is what the judges say it is;[10] but Americans further believe, in the words of Charles Warren, that, "however the Court may interpret the provision of the Constitution, it is still the Constitution which is the law and not the decision of the Court."[11] That consensus rejects the notion of Justice Frankfurter that our constant preoccupation with constitutional questions is a preoccupation of the American mind with a false value.[12] Of course constitutionality is not necessarily synonymous with wisdom; but the American consensus leans toward what is found to be constitutional with a heavy presumption in favor of its wisdom. Justice Frankfurter advised us to look for vindication of our most precious interests outside our courts of law. But Americans have refused to follow that advice. In spite of our record of violence, and in spite of occasional widespread displeasure with and even abuse of some Supreme Court decisions, Americans have chosen to live by the Rule of Law, and this I would take to be its commitment to the most basic of all human ideals. One must accept Kant's maxim that where legal justice is dead, life is no longer worth living; for Kant knew that without the Rule of Law there can be no justice, no morality, and no liberty.[13]

The Court, being a human construction, can make, and it has made, mistakes, several of which—most notoriously in the *Dred Scott* case and in *Plessy* v. *Ferguson*[14]—played mischievous roles in American history. No one claims for it, and it does not claim for itself, the transcendent quality of infallibility. The Court works within a self-correcting system: it has overruled itself by subsequent decisions in 150 instances.[15] And self-criticism is almost as common in the Court as is the exercise of the judicial function itself: for example, for the terms of 1972, 1973, and 1974, a total of 403 opinions of the Court were filed, but for the same period there were also filed 353 dissenting opinions;[16] in other words, for almost every opinion of the Court there was a dissenting opinion. The overruling decisions and the dissenting opinions have, I believe, in no way diminished the prestige and honor of the Supreme Court, but have rather, I think, over the years, contributed to the high and secure position the Court enjoys in national judgment and esteem.

So, too, the fact that the Jewish people accepted the teaching of the school of Rabbi Ishmael that "the Torah speaks in the language of men"[17] and that therefore there were bound to be differences of opinion over what the law is and requires, in no way weakened the halakhic (legal) hold over the mind and heart of the Jew. The classic sources record disputes over hundreds of laws. They record disputes between Hillel and Shammai, between Rav and Samuel, between Abbaye and Rava—what one school declared pure, the other declare impure. But the rabbis did not denigrate the controversies; on the contrary, all opinions were duly recorded, because the rabbis believed that the controversies were of lasting worth, for they were—unlike those of Korah and his followers—*mahaloket* (disputes) "for the sake of heaven." Unanimity of opinion, the rabbis declared, will not return until the coming of the Son of David. In his great work *The Sages: Their Concepts and Beliefs* (1975), Ephraim E. Urbach calls attention to the fact that the sages not only pointed out the errors in the decisions of other scholars, but that Rav Nahman, and after him Rava, several times announced publicly, "I erred in the statement that I made to you" (I, 618).

The spirit of the following passage from the *Aboth* according to Rabbi Natan, quoting a discussion by Rabbi Eliezar ben Azariah, is characteristic of American constitutional law as well as of Judaism:

> *Those that sit together in groups* are the scholars who come into (the academy) and sit down in groups; some forbid and others permit, some declare a thing unclean and others declare it clean, some pronounce a thing unfit and others pronounce it fit. Lest anyone say to thee, (in that event) I shall sit back and not study, Scripture declares, *They are given from one shepherd*: one God created them, one leader gave them, the Master of all things uttered them! Thou, too, therefore, make thine ear like a hopper and take in the words of them that forbid and the words of them that permit, the words of them that declare unclean and the words of them that declare clean, the words of them that pronounce unfit and the words of them that pronounce fit.[18]

In his recently published lectures, *The Role of the Supreme Court in American Government* (1976), Archibald Cox shares the fear, expressed by Justice Frankfurter, and before him by James Bradley Thayer, that "excessive reliance upon courts instead of self-government through democratic processes may deaden a people's sense of moral and political responsibility for their own future, especially in matters of liberty, and may stunt the growth of political capacity that results from the exercise of the ultimate power of decision" (p. 103). But the answer can be made that some of the most important reforming decisions of the Supreme Court in recent years have had precisely the opposite effect. In the reapportionment cases, in the cases which substantially restricted the law of libel in instances involving public officials or public figures, in the obscenity cases, in the cases freeing millions of Americans from every form of racial discrimination, in the cases recognizing and enforcing the right of privacy, the effect, I would say, has been, not to deaden but to enliven the "people's sense of moral and political responsibility for their own future, especially in matters of liberty," and not to stunt but to provoke "the growth of political capacity that results from the exercise of the ultimate power of decision"—decision by the private conscience of the individual citizen.

The Rule of Law and Executive Privilege: The Torah

The greatest test for the Rule of Law comes when the head of the state or government—king or president—asserts that he is beyond the reach of the law because of his divine right or his executive privilege. On this crucial matter we find that the Torah and the Constitution are identical in their approach and spirit.

Two of the most dramatic incidents recorded in the Bible show the firm Hebraic belief that the king can most certainly do wrong, and that he is accountable for his actions. In II Samuel we have recorded the shocking, criminal incident of the murder of Uriah on the order of King David, so that David might be free to take Bathsheba, Uriah's wife. The second incident, recorded in I Kings is about Ahab, king of Samaria, and how he let Jezebel, his wife, contrive the murder of Naboth, whose vineyard the king coveted. The two famous stories have strong features in common. In each, the king sought to take what did not belong to him, in one case another man's wife, in the other case another man's property. In each case the king contrived the murder of the person who stood in his way. In each case the king was held accountable by the prophet of his day: the prophet as the voice of God, the voice of conscience, the voice of outraged morality. The prophet, openly rebuking and condemning the shocking crime, served in place of our newspapers, our grand juries, our congressional investigating committees. The king of Israel, even David, could do wrong; unfortunately, most of the kings seemed to be more prone to do evil than to do good; with rare exceptions, they were a bad lot. But there was no whitewashing, no cover-up of their crimes.

The Talmud[19] records the famous confrontation between Simon ben Shetah and King Alexander Yannai (first century B.C.E.). The king was summoned one day before the Sanhedrin in connection with the case of his slave who had killed a man. The king came and sat down. Simon ben Shetah, who presided, said to the king: "Stand up, Yannai, and let the witness testify against you. For it is not before us that you stand, but before Him who spoke and the world came into being; as it is written, 'Then both the men between whom is the controversy shall stand' (Deuteronomy 19:17)." The king said: "It is not as you say, but as your colleagues will say." Apparently most of the members of the Sanhedrin were members of the Sadducean or the king's party, for when Simon turned to the right, his colleagues looked down at the ground, and when he turned to the left, they looked down at the ground. Then Simon ben Shetah said to them: "Are you full of thoughts [of expediency]? Let the Master of thoughts come and call you to account." (Incidentally, the dramatic tension in this story is intensified when one knows, as everyone involved in the scene knew, that the king was married to Salome Alexandra, the sister of Simon ben Shetah. But this fact only highlights the rugged independent character of Simon, who, though so highly placed, insisted on making his living by engaging in flax work.)[20]

As a consequence of the encounter between King Alexander Yannai and Simon ben Shetah, the rule came to be that the kings of Israel who were not of the house of David may neither judge nor be judged, may neither testify nor be testified against. The Sanhedrin made this rule in the light of what the rabbis considered to have been the historic experience, namely, that kings who were in the Davidic line would be good men and would comply with the demands of the Rule of Law: they would, when summoned, testify in the same way as any other witness, and when testified against, would not intimidate, harass, or persecute the witnesses. On the other hand, the rabbis considered the kings who were not in the line of David as being uniformly a very bad lot. For a court to tangle with such vicious kings could only bring the whole of the administration of justice into disrepute. It would, therefore, be prudent to exclude them from the reach of the legal order. Maimonides gives the following rationale for the rule laid down by the Sanhedrin: evil kings, said Maimonides, are arrogant, and if they were to be treated as commoners, the whole nation might be imperiled.[21]

For the good king, for whom there was no royal prerogative, there were many special laws devised to keep him humble and within the strict confines of the Rule of Law. Thus, as soon as he ascended the throne, he was required to write a scroll of the Torah for himself, which he was to have in addition to the copy left for him by his father, and one of the scrolls he was to have with him on all occasions and at all times, even as he sat down to eat. The king was forbidden to have more than a fixed number of wives, and if he added an extra one, he was to be flogged. He was forbidden to add even one horse to run before him in excess of the number fixed by law, and if he added an extra horse, he was to be flogged. He was forbidden to fill his private treasury, and if he did, he was to be flogged.[22]

The punishment hurt the pride and dignity of the king, but it at the same time enhanced the dignity of the law, and that, of course, was the law's objective. For the king was to set an example of how sedulously one should obey the law.[23]

The Torah was the supreme law of the land; and so, if the king issued a decree that contradicted a precept of the Torah, the decree was null and void, and no heed was to be paid to it;[24] for not even a prophet, let alone a king, may command adultery or murder or any other outrageously immoral or criminal act. Symbolic of the position of Judaism with respect to royal status is the rule that when there is an opportunity to ransom captives, the scholar was to be ransomed ahead of the king, for, the rabbis argued, anyone could be a king.

The basic principles of the Rule of Law, involving judicial

review of legislation and of executive action, are now being accepted by the State of Israel. As originally conceived, the Knesset was to be omnipotent, like the British Parliament, so that any statute enacted by the Knesset would be beyond judicial challenge or review. In the absence of a written constitution, the British example seemed to be a natural precedent. But now a constitution is evolving; there are already on the books four Basic Laws. It can be expected that a statute of the Knesset might be in conflict with one of the Basic Laws; but who is to say so, and how is the conflict to be resolved? The government has offered a bill that would vest in the Supreme Court the power to review legislation. When such a law is enacted and itself becomes a part of the written constitution, this aspect of the constitution of the State of Israel will reflect the spirit of the Torah, which puts some actions beyond the power of any human institution, regardless of its name and the high dignity with which it may be invested. And it will also reflect another model, modern and secular, to a consideration of which I now turn.

The Rule of Law and Executive Privilege: The United States Constitution

Fourteen years after the United States Constitution was adopted, the Supreme Court, in the famous case of *Marbury* v. *Madison*,[25] declared an act of Congress to be unconstitutional. This was no easy thing to do, for it was contended that since the three branches of government must be assumed to be coordinate and equal, Congress, which is vested with the lawmaking power, could determine for itself what the Constitution allows and prohibits. Congress would then be like the British Parliament: it would itself be the final arbiter of what is the law of the land by making the law of the land, which no court could unmake.

But Chief Justice Marshall and the Supreme Court took another line. The Constitution, they said, vests the judicial power in the Supreme Court and the lower federal courts. The function of a court is to apply the law to the facts of a case. But then the court must have the power *to say what the law is*. If we had no written Constitution, then the law would be what Congress declares is the law; but we *do* have a written Constitution, which states unambiguously that *it* is the *supreme* law of the land. If the Court should find that an act of Congress conflicts with a provision of the Constitution, the Court is bound to say that the Constitution, and not the act of Congress, is the law. It was settled in *Marbury* v. *Madison*, therefore, that it is "emphatically the province and duty" of the Court "to say what the law is"; the Court, therefore, has the power to reject an act of Congress as unconstitutional when the Court finds that congressional action conflicts with a provision of the Constitution.

As we can see, the principle of judicial review is but another term for the principle of the Rule of Law or of constitutional supremacy. It means that no governmental agency or official, in whatever branch of government, has any power to act except within the confines of the power delegated to the agency or the official by the Constitution and the laws validly adopted under it. Since *Marbury* v. *Madison*, as we have noted, the Supreme Court has held 99 acts of Congress unconstitutional.

Executive testing of the Rule of Law has been rare in American history. In a case decided in 1926, *Myers* v. *United States*,[26] the Supreme Court held that the Constitution vested all executive power in the President: except for the powers expressly delegated to Congress, the President of the United States could do almost anything that he considered to be in the public interest. And in *United States* v. *Curtiss-Wright Corp.*,[27] in 1936, the Court upheld the claim that the control of foreign relations was an exclusively executive function. "In this vast external realm," said the Court, "with its important, complicated, delicate and manifold problems, the President alone has the power to speak or listen as a representative of the nation." These two cases became the basis of the claim that the President enjoys, not constitutionally delegated, but inherent and unlimited executive powers. These decisions tended to place the President outside the principle of the Rule of Law, to make him, in the operation of the executive department and in the field of foreign affairs, as omnipotent as is the British Parliament in the field of legislation.

The first case to shake this line of precedents was the *Steel Seizure* case[28] of 1952. During the Korean War, when the steel industry faced the threat of a strike, President Harry S. Truman seized the factories. His theory was that after seizure the employees would be government employees and would not have the right to strike that private employees might have. No statute of Congress authorized the seizure, but the President claimed that he had the power as chief executive and also as commander-in-chief. The Court rejected this argument and held that the seizure was void. At least four of the Justices were influenced by the fact that Congress had adopted, in the Taft-Hartley Act, specific procedures for the government's intervention in strikes that were likely to create national emergencies, and these procedures did not include seizure of plants; on the contrary, Congress had considered and rejected a seizure provision. In any case, the decision of the Court marked the first important step in a substantial retreat from the claim of plenary presidential powers in the two earlier cases. In his opinion for the Court Justice Black said: "In the framework of our Constitution, the President's power to see that the laws are faithfully executed refutes the idea that he is to be a lawmaker."

It remained, however, for President Richard M. Nixon to present the clearest challenges to the Rule of Law. First was his claim that in cases involving domestic national security, the President had the power to order wiretapping or other forms of surveillance without regard to the limits imposed by the Fourth Amendment, which requires judicial action in the issuance of a warrant for the search or seizure of evidence—a court order that establishes definite limits of time and place and the things to be searched or seized, and proof that the search would be reasonable under the circumstances. The President claimed that he could act without regard for these constitutional requirements if in his judgment the surveillance would be in the interest of domestic national security. In a case decided in 1972, the Supreme Court unanimously held that such an order violated the Constitution and that prior judicial approval must be gotten by the President.[29]

An even clearer and more dramatic challenge from President Nixon came two years later. On March 1, 1974, a federal grand jury returned an indictment against seven defendants charging them with crimes relating to Watergate. Among those indicted were H. R. Haldeman, John D. Ehrlichman, John N. Mitchell, and Charles W. Colson. Richard M. Nixon was named as an unindicted co-conspirator. The Special Watergate Prosecutor asked Judge Sirica for a subpoena to obtain 64 Watergate tapes that were in the possession of the President. The judge issued the subpoena directing the President to produce the tapes. After releasing edited transcripts of some of the tapes, Nixon went before the judge to assert executive privilege to withhold the tapes and moved to quash the subpoena. Judge Sirica ruled that the court, and not the President himself, had the power to pass on the claim of executive privilege. The court, said Judge Sirica, would examine the tapes *in camera* and would pass on the claim of executive privilege in the light of the facts as they appeared to him. Nixon appealed this decision, and on July 24, 1974, the Supreme Court unanimously upheld the lower court's decision.[30]

Significantly, the Supreme Court relied on Chief Justice Marshall's opinion in *Marbury* v. *Madison*. In *United States* v. *Nixon* Chief Justice Burger followed closely the reasoned argument of Chief Justice Marshall. The trial court had had before it a criminal case. Justice requires the production of facts, that is, evidence both against and for the defendants. But how can a case proceed to proper judgment if the production of required evidence is frustrated by the claim of executive privilege? The President has, of course, executive privilege, *but only under the Rule of Law*. The claim and existence of privilege, said the Court, "must be considered in light of our historic commitment to the rule of law. . . . The ends of criminal justice would be defeated if judgments were to be founded on a partial or specu-lative presentation of the facts. The very integrity of the judicial system and public confidence in the system depend on full dis-closure of all the facts." Just as in *Marbury* v. *Madison* the Court held that, if justice is to be done, a court must have the power to decide *what the law is*, so in *United States* v. *Nixon*, by a parity of reasoning, the Court held that, if justice is to be done, a court must have the power to decide *what the facts are*.

There can be little if any doubt that Richard M. Nixon has inflicted some very serious wounds upon the American nation. But the record of history will show that as the wounds healed, a great benefit remained as a source of strength and glory. We know that sometimes even out of the carcass of a lion there may fly a swarm of bees and that out of it one may scrape honey, enough to eat and to share. *United States* v. *Nixon* is the honey out of the carcass of a lion.

I suggest that in some significant aspects the case of Rich-ard Nixon and that of King Alexander Yannai, though there is a span of some two thousand years between them, speak for the same ideals and principles. Although, on the facts, Yannai seemed to have successfully repulsed Simon ben Shetah and to have flagrantly escaped from the effectiveness of the Rule of Law, in the judgment of history the reverse is true. The names of Simon's craven colleagues, who valued their Sadducean par-tisanship more than the commandment of the Torah, are not even recorded, but history knows Simon ben Shetah as one of the greatest of the sages and reveres his name and memory for his courage, his uncorruptibility, and his vindication, even through seeming defeat, of the principle of the Rule of Law, of the principle that it is under God and His Law that the king reigns. The people remembered his life as a blessing and used to say that in the time of Simon ben Shetah rain fell so that the wheat came up as large as kidneys, barley like olive stones, and lentils like golden dinars.[31] He reaffirmed and tried, under the most difficult circumstances, to apply the principle as it is stated in Deuteronomy:

> And when he [the king] sits on the throne of his kingdom, he shall write for himself in a book a copy of this law [i.e., the Torah], from that which is in charge of the Levitical priests; and it shall be with him, and he shall read in it all the days of his life, that he may learn to fear the Lord his God, by keeping all the words of this law and these statutes, and doing them; that his heart may not be lifted up above his brethren, and that he may not turn aside from the commandment, either to the right hand or to the left; so that he may continue long in his kingdom, he and his children, in Israel.[32]

It is this principle that the Supreme Court, unlike the Sanhedrin when corrupted by the Sadducees, unanimously affirmed in an opinion written by a Chief Justice whom President Nixon had himself chosen.

The ways of Providence are incalculable. As Emerson noted, the road of Providence is often wild and rough, "and it is of no use," he added, "to try to whitewash its huge, mixed instrumentalities."[33] Because we are so deeply enshrouded in ignorance of the ways of Providence, we are commanded to say a benediction for a good fortune regardless of any consequent evil, and for misfortune regardless of any consequent good.[34]

3 /

Judaism and the Democratic Ideal

BASIC TO THE DEMOCRATIC IDEAL is the belief in equality. If a society is to be self-governing, the governing citizens must be assumed to be equally endowed for rights and duties. In modern history this belief in equality has contributed to cultural and religious pluralism; to constitutional government; to a fairly wide distribution of property; to universal education and emphasis on reason rather than superstition and force as instruments of social control and progress; to freedom of religion, speech, press, assembly, and association; and to equality of civil and political rights.

Just as a sharp distinction must be made between the accidental and the essential aspects of democracy, so the same distinction must be made among the various aspects of Judaism. Judaism, too, has had its highest insights, which, though they may have been conditioned by historical events, deserve perpetuation on their own account. On the other hand, like all other social institutions, Judaism has frequently needed to accommodate itself to the accidents of time and place in ways which did not at all times exhibit its own highest ideals. As in the case of democracy, it is the deeper motivation, the more profound insights, rather than the superficial aspects, that have kept Judaism alive as a way of life.

Living in the twentieth century, we, of course, face problems radically different from those faced by the prophets thousands of years ago, or by the great rabbis responsible for the Babylonian and Jerusalem Talmuds. Freedom of speech must mean something sharply different to a people with newspapers, radio, and television than it did to a people who prohibited reduction of their learning to writing. This means only that the branches of democracy are different; the root is the same: it is the same wherever and whenever people constitute a society. The problem of human freedom is always the same: though at one time, to achieve more of it, we must fight a civil war to abolish slavery; at another time we must fight to abolish racial distinctions in immigration policy; at one time, to achieve more of freedom, we must carry on a fight for women's suffrage; at another time the fight is against the white primary and the poll tax; at one time the fight is for freedom to teach the Torah in Javneh; at another time the fight is for freedom to teach the theory of evolution in Tennessee.

The scenes change; the characters and the plot are pretty much the same. This does not mean, necessarily, that the history of the human race can be written in terms of the history of liberty. All we mean to say is that whatever liberty may have meant at different times in the history of the human race, its essential character has been always pretty much the same. The struggles have been variations on a theme. The theme has been human equality and freedom.

When people are judged by any empirical test they are not equal: some are richer than others, some wiser, some swifter, some more beautiful. Yet the essence of democracy is equality. People reject the empirical tests and assert their equality, notwithstanding the evidence adduced by their eyes and ears and other senses. "All men are created equal," said Jefferson in the Declaration of Independence; and he had no footnote references to statistical tables by way of documentation. The belief in equality is a transcendental belief, if you wish; it makes an assertion which may be true only in the world of noumena. But no matter: it is the cornerstone of the democratic faith and the

essence of moral idealism. "The basis of democratic development," says Harold Laski, "is therefore the demand that the
system of power be erected upon the *similarities* and not on the
differences between men." Here we have the clue to the problem of democracy: differences are not to be eliminated, for it is
good that one man paints better than another, that one woman
writes better than does her neighbor, that one surgeon operates
better than another; yes, and even that one individual legislates
better than another.[1] But the system of power (political power,
economic and social power) must be based on the similarities
and not on the differences between human beings. The demand
for equality manifests itself in many relations: there is the demand for equal suffrage and for economic equality; there must
be no privilege by birth; there is the demand for educational
equality; there must be equality in participation in the results
of social developments and improvement; and there must be
equality before the law (real and not merely formal equality).

At bottom the democratic faith is a moral affirmation: men
are not to be used merely as means to an end, as tools; each is an
end in himself; his soul is from the source of all life; no matter
how lowly his origin, a man is here only by the grace of God—
he owes his life to no one but God. He has an equal right to pursue happiness; life, liberty, and the pursuit of happiness are his
simply by virtue of the fact that he is a live human being. He
has his place in the sun, and neither the place nor the sun was
made by men.

This faith finds its essence in what has been called the
"eminent dignity of human personality." One of the chief
sources of this faith is in the wellsprings of Judaism.

It may be possible to arrive at the philosophy of equality
within the framework of secular thought, as, for example, in the
systems of John Dewey and Bertrand Russell and in democratic
socialist Marxism. Within the framework of a religious system,
however, it is probably impossible to arrive at the philosophy of
equality in the absence of a belief in ethical monotheism.

For as long as one believes in the existence of a multiplicity of gods, each expressing his own biases and partialities, loving his friends and hating his enemies, there is no room for accommodation of the beliefs in the fatherhood of God and the brotherhood of man. In ethical monotheism, however, these beliefs are basic. Judaism conceived of God as the creator and ruler of the entire universe: "In the beginning God created the heavens and the earth."[2] He created Adam and Eve, from whom all mankind has sprung. Humanity lives, therefore, in "one world," one world in every sense of the term; the laws of physical nature are the same everywhere; the laws of human nature are the same everywhere: the heavens and the moral law are the same everywhere.

Not only are the physical laws the same everywhere, but the laws of righteousness too. For God is not only *ehad*, One, but He is God "sanctified in righteousness." He is the judge of all the earth, as Abraham said, and cannot act unjustly. "You are not a God who has pleasure in wickedness; evil shall not sojourn with You; You hate all workers of iniquity."[3] God, as the prophet said, wants to loose the fetters of wickedness, to undo the bands of the yoke, to deal bread to the hungry, to cover the naked, to shelter the homeless[4]—He wants to see all this, and more, accomplished—but through the free agency of man.

Implicit and explicit in the ethical monotheism that is Judaism are, then, the beliefs in the fatherhood of God and the brotherhood of man. Thus Malachi cried out: "Have we not all one Father? Has not One God created us?"[5] Thus is posited the fatherhood principle. But in the same breath the prophet added: "Why do we deal treacherously every man against his brother?" The fatherhood and brotherhood principles go together; they are inseparable[6]: if two men have the same father, are they, then, not brothers?

"God," said the rabbis, "is on the watch for the nations of the world to repent, so that He may bring them under His wings."[7] When the nations will accept the reign of righteousness, the Kingdom of God will have become established; and God wants this to happen above all else.

The most graphic expression of the fatherhood of God and the brotherhood of man is the statement in the Bible that man was created in the image of God.[8] The rabbis did not tire of creating homilies on this figurative expression of the oneness of the human family. Thus, as we have already noted, Rabbi Joshua ben Levi said: "When a man goes on the road, a troupe of angels proceed in front of him and proclaim, 'Make way for the image of the Holy One, blessed be He.'"[9]

In the Talmud the question is raised why man was created a solitary human being, why were there not created several Adams and several Eves at one time? The answer given is this: "So that it might not be said that some races are better than others."[10]

In the Midrash it is stated that the falling of rain is an event greater than the giving of the Torah, for the Torah is for Israel only, but rain is for the entire world.[11] According to the *Mekilta de-Rabbi Ishmael*, however, even the Torah is for the entire world: "The Torah was given in the wilderness and in fire and in water. As these three are free to all the inhabitants of the world, so are the words of the Torah free to all the inhabitants of the world."[12]

Are only the righteous among Israel the elect of God? Not at all; for righteousness, like sin, is the great leveler; the sinners among Israel are no better off than the evil ones among the non-Jews; and the righteous Israelites are not preferred to the righteous among the non-Jews. "The just among the Gentiles are the priests of God," say the rabbis.[13] "I call heaven and earth to witness that whether a person be Jew or Gentile, man or woman, manservant or maidservant, according to his acts does the Divine Spirit rest upon him."[14]

The injunctions in the Bible relating to the treatment of a brother were not construed as being directed only to the treatment of Israelites (though all Israelites are brothers) but of all mankind (for all men are brothers). Thus it was said: "The heathen is your neighbor, your brother. To wrong him is a sin."[15] The point is made graphically by the following incident related in the Midrash:

Simon ben Shetah was occupied with preparing flax. His disciples said to him, "Rabbi, desist. We will buy you an ass, and you will not have to work so hard." They went and bought an ass from an Arab, and a pearl was found on it, whereupon they came to him and said, "From now on you need not work any more." "Why?" he asked. They said, "We bought you an ass from an Arab, and a pearl was found on it." He said to them, "Does its owner know of that?" They answered, "No." He said to them, "Go and give the pearl back to him." "But," they argued, "did not Rabbi Huna, in the name of Rab, say all the world agrees that if you find something which belongs to a heathen, you may keep it?" Their teacher said, "Do you think that Simon ben Shetah is a barbarian? He would prefer to hear the Arab say, 'Blessed be the God of the Jews,' than possess all the riches of the world. . . . It is written, 'You shall not oppress your neighbor.' Now your neighbor is as your brother, and your brother is as your neighbor. Hence you learn that to rob a Gentile is robbery."[16]

In the same spirit, it is said in the Talmud that an idolator who studies the Torah is like the high priest; that a Gentile who lives a godly life is like the high priest.[17] It is related that Rabbi Judah told the Emperor Antoninus that he would have a share in the world to come even though he was a Gentile; for all men have a share in the world to come as long as they desist from acts of violence.[18] In the spirit of Simon ben Shetah the Talmud states: "In a city where there are both Jews and Gentiles, the collectors of alms collect both from Jews and Gentiles, and feed the poor of both, visit the sick of both, bury both, comfort the mourners whether they be Jews or Gentiles, and restore the lost goods of both."[19]

The Bible begins the story of man not with the birth of Abraham but with the creation of Adam and Eve; and the rabbis said that Adam was made from dust gathered by God from the four corners of the earth, so that no people should later be able to say that he was made from the dust gathered only in their own corner of the world. And wherever one turns in the writings of the Jews this motif of equality, the fatherhood of God and the brotherhood of man, appears irresistibly. Thus, at the Passover *seder* a drop of wine is to be spilled from the cup at the mention of each of the ten plagues with which the Egyptians were afflicted, the reason being, say the rabbis, that one's cup of joy cannot be full as long as there is suffering somewhere in the world. Again, at the *seder* the head of the household reads of the drowning of the Egyptian hosts in the Red Sea; and the rabbis comment on the passage by relating that when the drowning was taking place, angels in heaven commenced to sing the praises of the Lord, but He rebuked them, saying, "My children are drowning, and you would sing!"[20]

According to Isaiah, the Lord says: "Blessed be Egypt My people and Assyria the work of My hands, and Israel Mine inheritance."[21] And when Jeremiah speaks of the afflictions that must be visited upon the sinful people of Moab, he says that God weeps: "Therefore will I wail for Moab; yea, I will cry out for all Moab; for the men of Kir-heres shall my heart moan."[22] And the Book of Jonah, which occupies so prominent a place in Jewish ritual, relates God's concern for the salvation of the inhabitants of the city of Nineveh—a city of Gentiles, not of Jews.

Clearly, Judaism, or the ethical monotheism elaborated by the Hebrew Scriptures and the rabbis, posits as one of its fundamental precepts the equality of all men before God: all men who share righteousness share the grace of God.[23] This can be the case only if righteousness is not defined in terms of ritual observance, which, of course, is not expected of non-Jews, while works of benevolence are expected of everyone.

> Wherewith shall I come before the Lord?
> And bow myself before God on high?
> Shall I come before Him with burnt-offerings?
> With calves of a year old?

> Will the Lord be pleased with thousands of rams,
> With ten thousands of rivers of oil?
> Shall I give my first-born for my transgression,
> The fruit of my body for the sin of my soul?
> It has been told you, O man, what is good;
> And what the Lord requires of you;
> Only to do justly and to love mercy
> And to walk humbly with your God.[24]

That the ideals of equality and freedom which one finds at the heart of Judaism were not projected merely for "the end of days," but were principles of daily conduct, becomes clear when one examines some of the institutions characteristic of Judaism. In their relations with Gentiles the Jews speak of equality and freedom only as ends to be achieved after a long struggle: both the Jews and the non-Jews need to realize the nature of righteousness and strive for it together before they lie down together in equality, no one a lion and no one a lamb, but all children of the One Father, brothers who have issued from the same source of life. Through the long years the ideal was always there; Israel could preserve itself only by loyalty to its universalistic religion; its mission was never to be treated lightly, let alone forgotten; and every opportunity was to be taken advantage of to elicit from the non-Jew a blessing for the One God, and thereby to bring the non-Jew closer to righteousness. That is what *Kiddush ha-Shem* means. Awareness of this mission is illustrated by the dictum in the Talmud that to cheat a Gentile is even worse than to cheat a Jew, for besides being a violation of the moral law, such conduct brings Israel's religion into contempt and causes a *Hillul ha-Shem* (a desecration of the Name).[25]

In relations among themselves the Jewish people had an opportunity to give the ideal of equality "a local habitation and a name." The keystone of the Jewish community was the precept that "all Israel are responsible for one another." The rabbis relate that when Moses summoned all Israel before God, he said, "Your captains, your judges, your elders." But God made him add the words: "all the people of Israel." This passage receives clarification by the statement of the rabbis that Moses did not stop with "all the people of Israel," but went on to add: "your little ones, your wives, and the stranger that is in your camp"; for, said the rabbis, "God's mercies are on male and female alike, on the wicked equally with the righteous, as it says, 'From the hewer of your wood to the drawer of your water.' All are equal before God; hence it says, 'All the people of Israel.'"[26] Rabbi Akiba said that even the poorest in Israel are looked upon as freemen who have lost their possessions, "for they are the sons of Abraham, Isaac and Jacob."[27] In other words, *all men* are equal because all are the children of Adam and Eve; *all Israelites* are equal because all are the children of Abraham, Isaac, and Jacob.

The hereditary character of the priesthood in ancient Israel has led to the charge that Judaism recognized a class of privileged persons whose rights were obtained by birth: a hereditary aristocracy. But this belief is due to a misunderstanding. The priests were not permitted to consider themselves the heads of the community; they were a class whose status was determined by function; they were servants of God in a special sense; but being such servants, they carried obligations rather than privileges. People were not to stand in superstitious fear of them; they had no superior spiritual powers. The rabbis had freed themselves from almost every trace of sacerdotalism. The priesthood was maintained because the Torah required it; but it was not the priests who blessed Israel; it was God who bestowed the blessing; the priests were not intermediaries, like angels or saints: "It says at the end of the priestly benediction, 'and it is I that will bless them.' One might think from this statement that if the priests were to choose to bless the Israelites, then they were blessed, and if the priests did not choose, the Israelites were not blessed. Therefore it says, 'And it is *I* that will bless them. *I* will bless my people.'"[28]

Nor did the rabbis themselves constitute a privileged caste. Three crowns were recognized, the crown of the Torah, the crown of the priesthood, and the crown of the kingdom.

Aaron was worthy of the crown of the priesthood and obtained it, David was worthy of the crown of the kingdom and obtained it. The crown of the Torah remains, so that no man shall have the pretext to say: "If the crown of the priesthood and the crown of the kingdom were yet available, I would have proved myself worthy of them and have obtained them." For the crown of the Torah is available for all. For God says: "Of him who proves himself worthy of *that* crown, I reckon it to him as if all the three were yet available, and he had proved himself worthy of them all. And of everyone who does not prove himself worthy of the crown of the Torah, I reckon it unto him as if all three crowns were yet available, and he had proved himself worthy of none of them."[29]

The crown of the Torah is not inherited; it was worn by men who earned their living by cobbling shoes, weaving flax, or making candles.[30] A famous passage in *Pirke Aboth* is the following:

This is the way that is becoming for the study of the Torah: a morsel of bread with salt you must eat, and water by measure you must drink, you must sleep upon the ground, and live a life of trouble, the while you toil in the Torah. If you do thus, "Happy shall you be and it shall be well with you"; happy shall you be in this world, and it shall be well with you in the world to come. Seek not greatness for yourself, and crave not honor more than is due to your learning; and desire not the table of kings, for your table is greater than theirs, and your crown greater than theirs; and faithful is He, the master of your work, to pay you the reward of your labor.[31]

As water is priceless, said the rabbis, so is the Torah priceless; and as water is free for all, so is the Torah free to all. But the Torah was also compared to wine: as wine cannot keep in vessels of gold and silver, but only in cheap earthenware vessels, so the words of the Torah are preserved only in him who makes himself lowly.[32] "The greater the man," says the Midrash, "the humbler he is." Man, especially one who wears the crown of the

Torah, must be as humble as is God Himself; wherever you find the greatness of God, there, too, you will find his humbleness.[33] For "God loves nothing better than humility." Said Rabbi Johanan: "The words of the Torah abide only with him who regards himself as nothing." The Torah was not to be used as an ornament with which one might adorn himself, nor was it to be used as a spade with which to dig;[34] knowledge of the Torah was its own reward, for it is only to study the Torah that God created man: study of the Torah is his purpose, his end, his happiness, and his reward.[35] Nor may one charge fees for teaching the Torah; for the words of the Torah are free; God gave the Torah free: "he who takes a fee for the Torah destroys the world."[36]

The humility with which the greatest of the three crowns was to be worn is illustrated by the following incident related in the Talmud:

One day, at the close of the fig harvest, Rabbi Tarfon was walking in a garden, and he ate some figs which had been left behind. The custodian of the garden came up, caught him, and began to beat him unmercifully. Then Rabbi Tarfon called out and said who he was, whereupon they let him go. Yet all his days did he grieve, saying, "Woe is me, for I have used the crown of the Torah for my own profit." For the teaching ran: "A man must not say, I will study so as to be called a wise man, or rabbi, or an elder, or to have a seat in the college; but he must study from love. The honor will come of itself."[37]

The rabbis did not constitute a caste; they generally were not supported by the community but had to carry on a trade or calling from which they might support themselves and their families: "I call heaven and earth to witness," says the Midrash, "that every scholar who eats of his own, and enjoys the fruits of his own labor, and who is not supported by the community, belongs to the class who are called happy; as it is written, 'If you eat the fruit of your hands, happy are you.'" They were teachers, but received no compensation for their teaching; they had to make a living by spending a part of their day in some occupation for which there was a monetary reward: "He who occupies him-self with the study of the Torah only is as if he had no God."[38] A man was counseled to spend as little time as possible, how-ever, at his trade or work: only long enough to earn sufficient money to keep body and soul together. It was the duty of every-one to study the Torah at some time during each day: at least two ordinances in the morning and two in the evening; but the more study, the greater the reward (in the world to come).[39] "If a scholar engages in business and is not too successful, it is a good omen for him. God loves his learning and does not want to enrich him." The greatest calumny was to call one an *am ha-aretz* (a boor); to be poor was to be blessed, but to be ignorant was to be cursed. No *mitzvah* (commandment) was greater than study: the study of the Torah was superior to all other things—all other things except one: teaching the Torah. The commandment was: "Thou shalt teach them diligently to thy children."[40]

It is evident, then, that the crown of the Torah did not carry with it social privileges: the most learned man still needed to continue at his cobbler's bench or carpentry work. On the con-trary, it imposed the obligation to teach. The social ideal of Judaism was a community of scholars, where all would be com-panions. This is what it means to have been created in the image of God: to fulfill the obligation or commandment to study the words of God. This commandment was imposed on *every* Jew equally; it had to be fulfilled by himself, and not by a surrogate.

The schools were commanded not to engage in strife one with the other. Tolerance in scholarly dispute was an obligation. If a scholar has no *derekh eretz* (good taste, refinement), then he has no Torah.[41] It is related that Raba would open his discourse with a jest, and let his hearers laugh a little. For years the schools of Hillel and Shammai maintained a dispute over a mat-ter of law; finally a Voice descended in Javneh and cried out: "The words of both are the words of the Living God, but the decision should follow the School of Hillel." It was asked, why, if the words of both are the words of the Living God, was the decision granted to Hillel's school? The reply was: "Because the members of the school of Hillel are amiable of manner and courteous; they teach the opinions of both schools; and further-more, they always give the opinion of their opponents first."[42] This teaches, said the rabbis, that whoever abases himself is exalted by God. One was not to assume that the Divine Wisdom rested with him alone and that those who differed from him uttered words of no worth. One was to be a constant fount of tolerance and humility; one must be conscious of the relativity of his own statements even when, or perhaps especially when, the statement related to ultimate truths; for one was always subject to error and sin; all statements of truth were subject to finiteness and contingency. "One says its meaning is this, and another says its meaning is that. One gives such an opinion, his fellow a different one. But they all were given from one shepherd—that is from Moses, who received the teaching from Him who is One and unique in the world."[43]

Judaism is not merely a matter of beliefs and ceremonies, it is a way of life; and the economic aspect of human existence was not a matter of indifference to the prophets and rabbis. To-day we might be tempted to say that one aim was religious while the other was social; but Judaism would reject the distinction. Judaism recognizes no profane virtues; all virtues are sacred; the social function is as religious as the religious function is social. "Rabbi Judah said in the name of Rab; 'A man is forbid-den to eat anything until he has fed his beast.'"[44] Was this con-sidered a religious law or a social law? The distinction would not have been comprehensible to either Rabbi Judah or Rab. In Judaism all duties are divine commands. While some duties appear to be arbitrary, most are expressed in laws which con-science might recognize as obligatory on free will.[45] Economics and ethics are the same; ethics and religion are the same.

The study of the Torah was chiefly the study of social rela-tions, of individual and communal problems. The Torah taught that if your enemy needs help, you must help him;[46] and the same Torah taught that "he who gives food to a small child, must tell its mother"; and the same Torah taught that one must permit the poor to glean after the reapers, and that one must not take interest on a loan.[47]

Perhaps it was the experience of the Israelites in Egypt that compelled them to project the ideal of social equality and freedom. For in Egypt they saw that when great wealth and political power are in the hands of the same group, the welfare and happiness of the rest of the people are greatly imperiled. Political and economic power must be spread out among all, with little if any disparity in the distribution. If this is not accomplished, and men are unjustly exploited—used as mere means and not as ends; when it is forgotten that every man bears the image of God—physical, spiritual, and social pestilence will spread, and insurrection will follow, shaking the community to its very foundations. Masters cannot exploit their workers, and God not see the evil they do. The excessive wealth of the masters leads to luxury; when derived through injustice, wealth breeds further injustice; luxury corrupts what may have been left untouched by the injustice of exploitation. In the end the system collapses; blind injustice leans against the pillar of its palace and is destroyed with it.

Furthermore, as Charles Foster Kent pointed out, the experience of Moses showed him that violence does not avail in correcting industrial evils. The only true method is that which he used: "education and organization of those industrially oppressed; clear presentation of their claims and rights; patient, persistent agitation in order to educate public opinion; and efficient organization to protect their interests."[48]

The Israelites did not win their freedom merely to duplicate among themselves the system they had rejected. They were to build their own community on a basis of moral idealism, ethical religion, and social justice. There was to be in the Promised

Land no form of political or industrial oppression; for always the Jew was commanded, at every turn, in every crisis, at every temptation to commit an injustice, to "remember that you were a slave in the land of Egypt, and that the Lord your God brought you out from there by a mighty hand and an outstretched arm."[49] Future generations, after the Exodus, were commanded to look upon themselves as though *they*, and not merely their forefathers, had been rescued from the hand of the Egyptian taskmaster.[50] The *freshness* of their freedom was constantly to be before their eyes.

Moreover, they were commanded to remember in humility that it was not by their own strength that they won their freedom, but because God is One who watches over the poor, the fatherless, the afflicted, the helpless, the outcast: He is a just Judge; He loves justice and mercy and righteousness, and requites evil with evil.[51]

In ancient Israel the atmosphere was a thoroughly equalitarian one: all were practically equal and free. Each was represented in the council of the clan or tribe. While slavery was tolerated (it is to be remembered that the United States retained this institution until only four generations ago), the harshness of the master-servant relationship was in many ways mitigated. The Biblical fugitive-slave law, unlike the laws passed by Congress before the Civil War, protected the fugitive; for in Deuteronomy it is provided: "You shall not deliver to his master a bondsman that is escaped from his master unto you. He shall dwell with you in the midst of you, in the place which he shall choose within one of your gates, where he likes it best; you shall not wrong him."[52] While the institution of private property was recognized and there were laws against theft, clear recognition was given to the fact that property is fundamentally a social object, that property is subject to social control, that society may direct as to how much property a man may possess, how much of his income he may retain for his own use, for how long a period he may divest himself of title to property allotted to him, and so on. Thus it was provided that "when you come into your neighbor's vineyard you may eat grapes until you have enough at your own pleasure . . . when you come into your neighbor's standing corn, you may pluck ears with your hand."[53]

Among the first laws to protect the rights of laborers are those found in the Bible. The Sabbath was instituted as a social institution, as a day of rest, and "in it you shall not do any manner of work, you, nor your son, nor your daughter, nor your man-servant, nor your maid-servant, nor your ox, nor your ass, nor any of your cattle, nor your stranger that is within your gates."[54] Wages were to be paid promptly: "You shall not oppress a hired servant that is poor and needy, whether he be of your brethren, or of your strangers that are in your land within your gates. In the same day you shall give him his hire, neither shall the sun go down upon it; for he is poor, and sets his heart upon it; lest he cry against you to the Lord, and it be a sin in you."[55]

The well-off were forbidden to oppress the impoverished citizen: "No man shall take the mill or the upper millstone to pledge, for he takes a man's life to pledge. . . . When you do lend your neighbor any manner of loan, you shall not go into his house to fetch his pledge. . . . And if he be a poor man, you shall not sleep with his pledge; you shall surely restore to him the pledge when the sun goes down, that he may sleep in his garment, and bless you."[56] Bankruptcy laws were instituted, so that a man should not be borne down by his debts forever, but should, instead, have an opportunity for a fresh economic start: "At the end of every seven years shall you make a release";[57] the creditor shall not exact the debt from his debtor. At the same time, he who has must not close his heart to the importunities of him who has not, and say to himself that "the seventh year, the year of release, is at hand,"[58] and refuse to lend to the poor; for if this happen, God will hear the cry of the poor man, and the rich man will be guilty of a crime. "You shall surely give him and your heart shall not be grieved when you give unto him." [59] The owner of the land was not to think that the land was *really* his, to do with as he pleased; for the land is the Lord's; and the Lord commanded that every seventh year the land must lie fallow; it must not be abused, lest it become a waste place, and all the land a dustbowl. A share of a man's income had to be turned over to the communal authorities for the relief of needy persons. Even when a man built a house for himself, he was to take into consideration the duties he owes his neighbors: he must make a parapet for his roof, so that no one will fall from it. [60]

Time and again the prophets cried out against the economic inequalities that resulted in loss of freedom, injustice, and oppression. Men became too rich and too powerful for their own and the community's good. Such rich men were declared enemies of the people and the chief sinners against God. The accumulation of such wealth and the exploitation it entailed were condemned in the strongest terms possible:

Because they sell the righteous for silver,
And the needy for a pair of shoes,
You who trample the heads of the poor into the dust of the ground,
And turn aside the way of the humble. . . .
And they lay themselves down beside every altar,
Upon clothes taken in pledge,
And in the house of their God they drink
The wine of them that have been fined. [61]

Amos foretold such as these what their destiny would be:

Hear this word,
Ye kine of Bashan, that are in the mountains of Samaria,
That oppress the poor, that crush the needy,
That say to their lords, "Bring, that we may feast."
The Lord God has sworn by His holiness:

"Lo, surely the days shall come upon you,
That you shall be taken away with hooks,
And your residue with fish-hooks. . . ."[62]

Isaiah brought severe charges against the oppressors of the common man

Woe unto them that join house to house,
That lay field to field
Till there be no room and you be made to dwell
Alone in the midst of the land![63]

Just as Judaism posits the ideals of social equality and economic equality, so, too, it posits political freedom and equality. Israel was to be a holy nation, and each Israelite was to be a member of "a kingdom of priests, a holy nation." God alone is ruler over Israel. What need is there of a king? No one was permitted to make laws for the nation; for God had given His Torah to His people Israel—to every Israelite; there was no room left for a king. Not even David or Solomon could abrogate the laws of the Sabbath, or of the seventh year, or make just the oppression of the needy. Israel was different from all other peoples: its legislation came from God. If a king cannot make laws, of what use can he be? God was the Lawgiver, the Ruler, and the Judge. When the Jews asked Samuel to appoint over them a king, he told them of what use a king could be:

This will be the manner of the king that shall reign over you: he will take your sons and appoint them unto him for his chariots, and to be his horsemen; and they shall run before his chariots. And he shall appoint them unto him for captains of thousands, and captains of fifties; and to plow his ground, and to reap his harvest, and to make his instruments of war, and the instruments of his chariots. And he will take your daughters to be perfumers, and to be cooks, and to be bakers. And he will take your fields and your vineyards, and your oliveyards, even the best of them, and give them to his servants. And he will take the tenth of your seed, and of your vineyards, and give to his officers, and to his servants. And he will take your men-servants, and your maid-servants, and your goodliest young men and your asses, and put them to his work. He will take the tenth of your flocks; and you shall be his servants.[64]

The Jews never forgot this lesson of Samuel's; even though they took upon themselves the yoke of a kingship, they would not tolerate oppression and despotism. The king was to be a servant of the people and not their master; he was to rule under God and not as a substitute for Him. Thus the Jews became a "rebellious" people; for they would not tolerate a tyrant even if he were of the seed of David. When Solomon died, the northern tribes rose in protest against a perpetuation of oppressive measures by Rehoboam, whom Solomon had nominated as his successor. It is related that Rehoboam and the Israelites met at Shekhem, where he was asked if he would make lighter their yoke. The king took counsel with the old men who had served Solomon, and they said to him: "If you will be a servant unto this people this day, and will serve them, and answer them, and speak good words to them, then they will be your servants forever."[65] The king would not follow their advice; he "gave no heed to the people." When the Israelites saw that he disregarded their petition, they said to him:

> We have no portion in David
> Neither have we inheritance in the son of Jesse;
> Everyman to his tents, O Israel.[66]

Even if it meant breaking up the kingdom, Judaism's democratic ideals had to be asserted and reasserted. Thus it was throughout Israel's history in Palestine. The people, and sometimes the prophets speaking for the people, constantly submitted the moral presuppositions of the ruling caste to scrutiny and reexamination. The freedom of the private moral judgment was always kept alive. When Ahab, misguided by Jezebel, his queen, showed his disloyalty to the democratic ideals, a popular uprising ended his dynasty. Elijah spoke for the conscience of

Israel. When Naboth refused to sell his vineyard to the despotic king, and the king and queen, through a perversion of justice, had him murdered, Elijah spoke out against the king, and when the king heard his words, "he rent his clothes and put sackcloth upon his flesh and fasted, and he lay in sackcloth, and went softly."[67] For the king knew that he could reign only under and within the law; and he was not above the Torah.

And this brings us to our final point, namely, that no people can be free, no democracy can continue to exist, if the rulers selected by the people do not consider themselves bound by the law. There must be limitations on rulers if the individual's rights are to be preserved. The citizen's rights are measured by the restrictions on government. There must, in other words, be a constitution which defines how far the government may go in this matter or that delegated to its authority. Israel had such a constitution in the Torah. No one was above it. Only under the Torah could kings rule and judges judge. As God is righteous, so must the king be; as God defends the weak, so must the king. Only justice is the foundation of a people's happiness and stability. Psalm 72 expresses this thought:

> Give the king Your judgments, O God,
> And Your righteousness unto the king's son;
> That he may judge Your people with righteousness,
> And Your poor with justice. . . .
> May he judge the poor of the people,
> And save the children of the needy,
> And crush the oppressor. . . .
> He will have pity on the poor and needy,
> And the souls of the needy he will save.
> He will redeem their soul from oppression and violence.

This, in part, is the picture of the ideal king.

Indeed, how could Israel view the status and function of government otherwise; for does not God Himself govern in accordance with law? Judaism is a law-centered religious civilization. All that God does, said Rabbi Akiba, He does by justice; "the procedure in the heavenly court is governed by law as in an earthly court."[68] The day has twelve hours, said Rabbi Judah in the name of Rab, and in the first three God sits and busies Himself with the Torah. God Himself is bound by the Torah, by His own laws. He made the world "by law," not arbitrarily.[69] Why, then, should He not spend His time teaching the Torah to the righteous in heaven? When Moses went up to heaven, he found God sitting and weaving crowns for the letters of the Torah, little flourishes on some letters of the Torah to ornament the Scroll of the Law.[70] The imagination of the Jewish folk could devise no occupation more worthy of God than the writing and study of His own Torah, because the Jew himself found such a delight in the law: "But his delight is in the law of the Lord; and in His law does he meditate day and night."[71]

The ordinances of the Lord are to be desired more than gold; they are sweeter than the honey and the honeycomb. "I have rejoiced in the way of Your testimonies. . . . I will delight myself in Your statutes."[72] The Lord's commandments apply to every significant act in life; as Rabbi Phineas said, one must think of the commandments when one builds a house, when he makes a door, when he buys new clothes, when his hair is cut, when his field is plowed, when his field is sowed, when the harvest is gathered, "even when you are not occupied with anything, but just taking a walk. . . ."[73] And the commandments are for *all* the people to observe: "All are equal before the law. The duty of observance is for all. For the Torah is the 'inheritance of the congregation of Jacob.' It does not say 'priests' or 'Levites' or 'Israelites,' but 'the congregation of Jacob.'"[74]

No one can be above the Rule of the Law—whether he wear the crown of the Torah, or the priestly crown, or the royal crown —because all men are equal, all are equally bound by the Law and subject to it, alike at every point; more than this, the world itself is subject to the Law; God made the world in accordance with the Law. Is not then even God Himself bound by the Law?

"God created the world by the Torah: the Torah was His hand-maid and His tool by the aid of which He set bounds to the deep, assigned their functions to sun and moon, and formed all nature. Without the Torah the world falls."[75] The same Torah sets bounds to man's greed, man's injustice; assigns functions to this man and that, and forms civilization.

Without law there is no freedom. Unless a people meditate on the statutes and delight in the law, they will not be able to walk at ease; unequal strength will lead to unequal justice. If Judaism projects a *rechtlichbuergerliche Gesellschaft*, it is to be borne in mind that this law-centered society is also an *ethisch-buergerliche Gesellschaft*, for the law is within as well as without; and at the center of the ethico-legal system is the injunction of God: "For unto Me are the children of Israel slaves; they are not slaves unto slaves."[76]

Not all democratic institutions were foreseen by the prophets and rabbis; such agencies are evolved by societies of men, as the need for them is felt to be irresistible even by those who would prevent their emergence. But the spirit, the inner values, the energies of democracy are right at the very heart of Judaism.

4 /

Conscience: *The Movement*
from Duty to Right
—from the Bible to the Bill of Rights

I

IN THE FIRST CHAPTER of Exodus it is related that
the new ruler of Egypt, alarmed by the increase in the number
of Israelites, spoke to the "Hebrew midwives" and directed
them to kill all male infants born to Hebrew women. "But the
midwives feared God," the Bible goes on to relate, "and did not
as the king of Egypt commanded them, but saved the men-children alive."[1] Thereupon the king issued a new decree, directed
not to the midwives but to the people generally, who were
ordered to kill all new-born Hebrew males by throwing them into the river Nile.[2]

These events, which may have happened some thirty-four
hundred years ago, relate to what may well be the first recorded instance in history of what is today called nonviolent
civil disobedience.

From the Biblical text it is not clear whether the midwives
were themselves Hebrews; for they acted as they did, not be-

cause they were Hebrews, but because they "feared God." The text twice mentions the fact that they "feared God" or, as we say today, that they listened to the voice of conscience rather than to the law of the state or the voice of the king.

In the first book of Samuel there is another clear and dramatic instance of nonviolent civil disobedience. It is related that when King Saul learned that a certain priest had given David food and other assistance, he ordered the priest to appear before him and decreed his death and the death of all his kin. The crucial words of the Biblical text are as follows: "And the king said to the guards who stood about him, 'Turn and kill the priests of the Lord; because their hand also is with David, and they knew that he fled, and did not disclose it to me.' But the servants of the king would not put forth their hand to fall upon the priests of the Lord."[3]

This may be the first recorded instance of nonviolent civil disobedience by military men refusing to obey superior orders. It is not clear why the men of the guard refused to lay hands on the priests and their families, whether because the victims belonged to the priestly class, or because they were civilians. Whatever the reason, their action was a clear case of civil disobedience.

In the book of Daniel we find perhaps the first recorded instances of what became a pattern of Jewish life and history, namely, the willing submission to martyrdom for the sake of one's religion. Chapter 3 records that Nebuchadnezzar erected a huge image of gold and sent out a summons to all the high officials of the realm to attend the dedication; he issued an order that when they heard the sound of music they were to prostrate themselves and worship the image, and that whoever disobeyed this command would be thrown into a blazing furnace. It was later reported to the king that three Jews—Shadrach, Meshach, and Abednegó—who were high provincial administrators, had failed to worship the golden image. When charged by the king with this offense, they said to him: "We have no need to answer you on this matter. If there is a god who is able to save us from the blazing furnace, it is our God whom we serve, and He will save us from your power, O king; but if not, be it known to your majesty that we will neither serve your god nor worship the golden image that you have set up."[4]

Chapter 6 relates that Darius the king had appointed Daniel chief of his officers. The officers then conspired to bring about the fall of Daniel, and to this end they contrived an ingenious trap. They induced Darius to issue a decree that for thirty days no man was to offer petition to any man or god except to the king, on pain of death in the lion's den. Daniel, however, went on to pray (that is, to petition) to God three times daily, with the window of his chamber open toward Jerusalem. His enemies came upon Daniel when he was thus petitioning God rather than Darius, and then went with their report to the king. After trying to find a way out, the king felt compelled to order his law enforced, and Daniel was put into the den of lions.[5]

This case of Daniel, it should be noted, differs from our three previous instances in two important respects: (a) In the case of the Egyptian midwives, in the case of Saul's guards, and in the case of the three Jewish officials, there was simply a refusal to commit an act which was deeply felt—by the persons ordered to perform it—to be inconceivable. In the case of Daniel, however, there was a positive act: he did not merely *refuse* to perform an act; he *performed* an act in violation of a law. (b) The first two cases involved moral conscience—refusal in the face of orders to commit murder. In the cases reported in the book of Daniel, however, we have acts that are not in the realm of the moral conscience but in the realm of religious worship. While these differences are significant, the concept of nonviolent civil disobedience is broad enough to accommodate such actions as well as additional types of conduct.

The four books of Maccabees in the Apocrypha offer numerous instances of civil disobedience during the period of the Hellenization of Judea, when the second Temple was defiled and was dedicated to Zeus. Some Jews assisted in the work of Hellenization and even in the persecution of fellow Jews who tried to obstruct the process. The Syrian overlords forbade the Jews to offer sacrifices or to observe the Sabbath and festivals. The Jews were compelled to make and to worship idols, to sacrifice swine, and to leave their sons uncircumcised; and disobedience meant death. But I Maccabees records that "nevertheless, many in Israel were firmly resolved in their hearts not to eat unclean food. They preferred to die rather than be defiled by food and break the holy covenant, and they did die."[6] When the king's officers came to Modiin, to enforce the decrees against religious observances, Mattathias answered them in these resounding words: "Yet will I, my sons and my brothers, walk in the covenant of our fathers. . . . We will not listen to the decrees of the king by going astray from our worship, either to the right or to the left."[7] And then he issued his call: "Let everyone who is zealous for the Law, and would maintain the covenant, follow me."[8]

The second book of Maccabees records many dramatic instances of martyrdom when Jews resorted to civil disobedience: women who had violated the law on circumcision were hurled from the city wall with their infants held to their breasts; men who had secretly observed the Sabbath day in caves were burned alive.

The second and fourth books of Maccabees relate the story of the martyrdom of a mother and seven brothers who refused to eat forbidden food that was associated with idolatrous sacrifices. The position of nonviolent civil disobedience is stated unambiguously by them as they cry out to the king's officers: "It is certain that we are ready to die rather than transgress the laws of our fathers."[9] The seven brothers, who were called Maccabees by the church, became models for Christian martyrs; and though the rabbis rejected the books of the Apocrypha from the canon of Sacred Scripture, they, too, make a great deal of the story of the seven brothers.[10]

What may be the first recorded instance of mass nonviolent civil disobedience is found in Josephus' *The Jewish War*.[11] It revolved around the decision of Caligula (referred to as Caius) to place his statue in the Temple in Jerusalem. He appointed Petronius as his agent. Petronius was given a large army, but was instructed to try, in the first instance, to persuade the Jews to permit the installation of the statue peacefully. If, however, the Jews were to refuse, then Petronius was to move with his army and install the statue by force. Petronius prepared an army of Romans and auxiliaries to carry out this mission, and in due course arrived at Acre (referred to as Ptolemais). What happened after that is graphically reported by Josephus:

> But there came ten thousands of the Jews to Petronius at Ptolemais to offer their petitions to him that he would not compel them to violate the law of their forefathers. "But if," they said, "you are wholly resolved to bring the statue and install it, then you must first kill us, and then do what you have resolved on. For while we are alive we cannot permit such things as are forbidden by our law and by the determination of our forefathers that such prohibitions are examples of virtue."
>
> Petronius, however, was angry at them, and said: ". . . Caesar has sent me. I am compelled to observe his decrees. . . ." Then the Jews replied: "Since, therefore, you are so disposed, O Petronius, that you will not disobey Caesar's orders, neither will we transgress the commands of our law. . . ."
>
> When Petronius saw by their words that their determination was hard to be removed, and that . . . he would not be able to be obedient to Caius in the dedication of his statue, and that there must be a great deal of bloodshed, he took his friends and servants and hastened to Tiberias, to see how the Jews there felt about the affair; but many ten thousands of Jews met Petronius again when he came to Tiberias. . . .
>
> Then Petronius said to them [at Tiberias]: "Will you then make war with Caesar, regardless of his great preparations for war and your own weakness?" They replied: "We will not by any means make war

with Caesar, but we will die before we see our laws transgressed." Then they threw themselves down on their faces and stretched out their throats and said that they were ready to be slain. And this they did for forty days, neglecting to till their soil, though this was the season which called for sowing. Thus they continued firm in their resolution and proposed to die willingly rather than see the statue dedicated.

When matters were in this state . . . Petronius determined to listen to the petitioners in this matter. He called the Jews together in Tiberias, who came many ten thousands in number. . . . Said Petronius: "I do not think it just to have such a regard to my own safety and honor as to refuse to sacrifice them for your preservation, who are so many in number and who endeavour to preserve the regard that is due to your law. . . . I will, therefore, send to Caius and let him know your resolutions, and I will assist your cause as far as I am able, so that you may not suffer on account of your honest designs, and may God assist you. . . . But if Caius should be angry and turn the violence of his rage on me, I would rather undergo that danger and affliction on my body or soul than see so many of you perish. . . ."

When Petronius had said this and had dismissed the assembly of Jews, he asked the principal men among them to look after their fields, to speak kindly to the people and to encourage them to have hope. . . . He then wrote to Caius . . . to entreat him not to drive so many ten thousands of these men to distraction; that if he were to slay these men, he would be publicly cursed for all future ages.

Philo, recording the same incidents, reports the Jewish plea to Petronius in essentially the same words as those of Josephus. The core of the plea, according to Philo was in the following words.:

We are evacuating our cities, withdrawing from our houses and lands. . . . We should think ourselves gainers thereby, not givers. One thing only we ask in return for all, that no violent changes should be made in this temple. . . . But if we cannot persuade you, we give up ourselves for destruction that we may not live to see a calamity worse than death. We hear that forces of cavalry and infantry have been prepared against us if we oppose the installation [of the image of Caesar]. No one is so made as to oppose a master when he is a slave. We [therefore] gladly put our throats at your disposal.[12]

II

Leaving out for the moment the incidents from the book of Daniel, the Biblical instances of civil disobedience that we have cited—the case of the Egyptian midwives and that of Saul and his guards—involved orders to commit murder. The cases cited from the books of Maccabees and from Josephus involved orders to commit the sin of idolatry. Now a man of conscience may readily agree that he would prefer martyrdom rather than commit murder or practice idolatry. But what of laws or decrees that call for acts not so heinous as murder or idolatry though against the conscience? In the course of the war that Hadrian waged to destroy Judaism and the Jewish nation, countless Jews stood ready for martyrdom. But the rabbis saw that indiscriminate martyrdom might itself be a peril to Jewish survival. With this consideration before them, the rabbis decreed that the duty to prefer martyrdom should be restricted to three transgressions: murder, idolatry, and incest. The rabbis attached this legal principle to Leviticus 18:5, which reads as follows: "And ye shall guard my statutes and my ordinances, by doing which a man shall *live*." They conclude from this passage that the Torah was given to enhance life rather than to induce death. The emphasis of the Torah is on holy living and not on holy dying. The rabbis also pointed to the fact that the passage stated that the statutes and ordinance are such that by observing them "a man" shall live—not an Israelite, but "a man." With these two highly significant interpretations in mind, the rabbis felt that martyrdom had to be limited to instances that involved laws that transgressed the most basic principles of what came to be called natural law. (There can hardly be any question about murder and incest falling into this category.[13] Idolatry was so closely associated with grossly immoral practices that it could rank with the transgressions of the basic precepts of natural law, and that association was made and stressed by the prophets of the Bible and the rabbis of the Talmud.)

The *locus classicus* of the legal formulation of the principle concerning martyrdom is the Talmud:

> From every law of the Torah the rule is that a man may transgress the commandment rather than suffer death—excepting idolatry, incest and murder. . . . Murder may not be committed [even] to save one's life. . . . For example, someone came to Raba and told him: "The general of my town has ordered me to go and kill a named person, and if not, the general will kill me." Raba said to him: "Let the general kill you rather than that you should commit murder. Who knows that your blood is redder? Maybe his blood is redder!"[14]

In the face, then, of orders, or laws, that command idolatry, incest, or murder, the above-stated halakhic principle calls for civil disobedience—as a *duty*—even at the cost of one's life.[15]

Now, what of the incident involving Daniel? As the story is related, Daniel was not called on to perform any act at all. If he had not petitioned (prayed) at all for thirty days, he would have complied with the king's decree. Why, then, did he resort to civil disobedience? Was his conduct consistent with the legal principle later formulated by the rabbis?

It seems that the incident may be interpreted consistently with the above principle. The Persians believed that their king was a god; accordingly, they set a trap for Daniel, for they suspected that he would refuse to pray to the king as one prays to God. Had Daniel failed to offer prayers to anyone for thirty days, his enemies could have used this as evidence of a rejection by him of a belief in the king as a divinity. From this point of view, the story in its essentials is not significantly different from the story in Josephus of Caligula's desire to have his statue installed in the Temple on Mount Moriah. By praying to God while looking out the window that faced toward Jerusalem, Daniel acted out his rejection of Persian idolatry. Accordingly, the story of Daniel is not only an instance of civil disobedience, but it is also an instance of the later legal formulation of the *duty* of civil disobedience to avoid the commission of idolatry, incest, or murder.

III

The relationship in classical Jewish thought between law and conscience—conscience in which civil disobedience is rooted—is extremely subtle and complex.[16] For the purposes of the present discussion we shall limit our exploration of this matter to three aspects:

(a) Conscience, as a specific concept, does not appear in the Hebrew Scriptures. It is, however, clearly implied. The story of Cain and Abel would have no point unless conscience were assumed; for there had been no supernatural revelation of a law against murder before one brother killed the other, nor was there at that time an enacted criminal code. The same may be said of the judgment on Sodom and the other cities of the plain; and so, too, of Noah and the judgment on his generation; and so, too, of the judgments on Egypt and on the people of Canaan. Much of the Bible, including many passages of the prophets, assumes that there are laws written on the tablets of the heart, that there is a law in the heart.[17]

The words of Jeremiah, "I will put my law in their inward parts, and in their hearts will I write it,"[18] were not only a promise but also a statement of basic belief as to the nature of man. Without this belief in a law written by God on the tablets of the heart of every person, God could not be the judge of all the universe, of all peoples and nations. Without this belief, God would be only the tribal God of Israel, and he could not have been their judge before the revelation of the Ten Commandments at Sinai; without this belief, the commandments not to kill, not to commit adultery, or not to commit theft would have binding force only on Israel. Indeed, it may be argued that the conception of *man* made in the image of God means primarily that *man* is made with a moral conscience—and with the freedom to act against its commands. It is this that the Bible means when it states that the Egyptian midwives "feared God"; that Amalek, when he acted cruelly, showed that "he feared not God";[19] that Abraham pretended to be the brother of Sarah, because when they came to Gerar he thought: "Surely the fear of God is not in this place; and they will slay me for my wife's sake."[20]

Indeed, in Biblical contemplation, there may be said to be a special category of sin which is an act committed "against the Lord," that is, a sin which implies the denial of the existence of God, or atheism. This applies to a wrong done to another person secretly, under circumstances where there are no witnesses— no witnesses but God. In Leviticus this type of sin is referred to as follows: "If any one sin, and commit a trespass against the Lord, and deal falsely with his neighbor in a matter of deposit, or of pledge, or of robbery, or have oppressed his neighbor; or have found that which was lost, and deal falsely therein, and swear to a lie in any of all these that a man doeth, sinning therein, . . ."[21] Rabbi Akiba attached great significance to the phrase "against the Lord," for he believed it points up the fact that the guilty man denies that God was a witness to the deposit or the other acts, and thus by implication he denies God's existence or presence. This, it seems to me, gives the phrase in Leviticus the same meaning as the phrase "feared God," and it is a meaning based on what we generally speak of as conscience.

It was with such views in mind, and especially the story of Noah and the flood, that the rabbis of the Talmud formulated what they called "the seven commandments given to the descendants of Noah."[22] These commandments prohibit idolatry, murder, theft, incest, blasphemy, and the eating of flesh taken from living animals, and require the establishment of courts of justice. How were these seven commandments "given" and to whom? They were "given" on the "tablets of the heart," and to every person everywhere, since Noah was a kind of second Adam. These commandments spell out, therefore, a natural law, a law binding on the conscience of every person, and from which no man or woman, nation, or generation can claim exemption.

(b) This principle of a law of nature, elaborated into the seven commandments given to the descendants of Noah, is obviously the source from which the Jewish tradition selected the three-part principle of civil disobedience: that a man must choose to die, if necessary, rather than obey a law or decree that he commit murder, incest, or idolatry.

One significant aspect is that the duty of civil disobedience is not extended to all of the seven commandments but only to these three. Thus, if the order is to commit, for example, theft, on the pain of death, the person should commit the theft.[23]

Suppose that the sanction for a refusal to commit theft, however, is imprisonment, not death. May a person, then, resort to civil disobedience and choose to go to prison rather than commit the wrong? The principle is silent as to such cases. The principle only states *explicitly* that one *must* choose to suffer a wrong rather than commit it when the wrong to be committed is idolatry, incest, or murder. And the principle *implies* only that when the wrong to be suffered is *death* as a penalty, one *must* commit the wrong ordered—except idolatry, incest, or murder —and avoid death. A great deal is, therefore, left open—when the wrongs commanded are other than the three cardinal ones, or when the penalty threatened for disobedience is something other than death. Exploration of this open territory is beyond the reach of this essay.

(c) Finally, our discussion should have demonstrated the distinctly Jewish, halakhic approach to the problem of conscience *versus* law that is an expression of the genius of classical, normative Judaism. The legal order provides a constitutional or *higher law* by which a person is commanded to disobey certain orders, even when they are made by the king or other high officers of the state. Halakhic Judaism thus speaks not of a right, but of a *duty*, a *legal duty*, of *civil disobedience*. Thus, while it recognizes conscience, or "the fear of God," or the laws written on the tablets of the heart, it converts morality into law by demanding that, given proper circumstances, the *higher law* becomes the living law—a living law that contradicts, and even nullifies, the enacted law—or what wrongly pretends to be the law.

The dialectic of the conceptual relationship between the demands of conscience (or of the inner or natural law) and those of enacted law or orders of the state, is probably impossible to express with any precision, or in terms of logical consistency. The ancient Jewish authorities were wise not to make the attempt but instead resorted to existential terms by conjuring up the case of the governor of the town ordering X to go and kill Y. What did Raba say to X? "Let the governor slay you rather than that you should commit murder. Who knows that your blood is redder? Perhaps Y's blood is redder than yours." Thus, as is often the case in Hebraic-rabbinic thought, an example symbolizes a principle,[24] the commentary becomes the text—as if there were a fear of making the word into a thing, of accepting the notion that in the beginning was the *Logos*, the word. For the ultimate sanctity is life, God's creation, and not what is said about it in some abstract formula. Yet life, sacred as it is, is given and sustained for certain ends. If these ends are threatened—by coerced idolatry, immorality, or "the shedding of blood"—life becomes worthless and must well be given up. But the ends are such only because they enhance life. It is "holy living" and not "holy dying" that is sought and hoped for and cherished.

The unsympathetic critic may say that we have constructed a rather heavy and imposing superstructure on a meager foundation of small incidents, like that of the Egyptian midwives and Saul's bodyguards. Until our own tumultuous days, one would not have thought of such incidents as implying and foreshadowing a principle so momentous for the human spirit as that of civil disobedience. But often it takes many centuries and a great deal of history to disclose the existence of an ideal, a theory, or principle. In the Preface to his *Poems* (1853 edition), Matthew Arnold glibly wrote that "an action like the action of the Antigone of Sophocles, which turns upon the conflict between the heroine's duty to her brother's corpse and that to the laws of her country, is no longer one in which it is possible that we should feel a deep interest."

One may be sure that when read in 1853 this judgment seemed to be eminently to the point. But would Arnold have made this judgment after the Nürnberg tribunal judgments, after the other many war-crime trials, after the Eichmann trial? Would he have made this judgment in the light of Gandhi's civil disobedience struggle to end untouchability in India? Would he have made this statement in the 1960's in the light of the lunch-counter sit-ins led by Martin Luther King, Jr.? Indeed, in the 1960's perhaps more people read or saw *Antigone* as written by Sophocles or in the version prepared by Anouilh than in the hundred years from 1853.

Great actions, whether they be those of a young, bereaved girl, or of midwives, or of young soldiers engaged to protect their king, have a way of surviving the ravages of time, and demonstrate, when the time is appropriate, their relevance and significance for that which is "permanent in the human soul." That demonstration can be made by Antigone or Socrates, by Thomas More or Bronson Alcott or Thoreau, by Gandhi or Martin Luther King, Jr., or by thousands of nameless Jews not afraid of a Roman general nor of the Roman Emperor who sent him, nor of death, but who did have the "fear of God"—a "fear" that gives boundless courage to a spirit that suddenly discovers itself as boundless. These men and women found it easy to act but impossible or difficult to give a rational account of their actions. But this is natural, for conscience demands that the act be justified before God, and not necessarily before other human beings; God knows the heart, and its inner thoughts and secrets.

And God does not demand great sacrifice when the occasion

is not one of transcendent importance; God makes His demands only when man is called upon to perpetrate murder or commit immorality or idolatry. Only then does the law of God demand violation of the law of man at the cost of one's life. Civil disobedience is not offered as an everyday method for meeting unwelcome situations, for the ameliorations of which society and individuals must find other methods and agencies.

Beyond this, however, Jewish tradition, as we have seen, places the highest value on martyrdom as the price that is paid for defiance of a tyrant whose policy it is to destroy the Jewish religion. In the solemn service of Yom Kippur, a prominent place is given to a recital of the heroism and martyrdom of the ten great scholars who, during the Hadrianic persecutions, steadfastly refused to accept the prohibitions on observances and the ban on the study of the Torah. At the risk of their lives they acted in defiance of imperial edicts and gladly suffered torture and death in order to sanctify the Name of their God (*Kiddush ha-Shem*). Within the Jewish tradition of nonviolent civil disobedience, these ten martyrs have played a role, in the education of the Jewish conscience, that is at least comparable to that of Socrates for Western society: the role of witnesses to the force of the moral and religious conscience and its imperious claims to obedience—claims that are more pressing than those of any state or emperor.

IV

The Rule of Law is of supreme importance, but it must not be allowed to become an absolute; our respect for it must not become the worship of an idol. For there are occasions when moral claims become superior to the commands of the state. Jewish law, as we have seen, took into itself these moral claims and converted them into legal duties, so that civil disobedience itself became lawful and was operative within the Rule of Law.

The resolution of the difficult conceptual problems became possible perhaps through emphasis on the concept of *duty*. It was not a question of what a person might or might not subjectively wish to do. It was not a question of a clash between the commands of the state and the rights of the person. It was not a question of the *right* of civil disobedience. It was always a matter of facing and performing one's *duty*: the *duty* not to kill, the *duty* not to commit an immoral act, the *duty* to avoid any form of idolatry. It was not a question of what one's conscience dictated, but what the law—the Higher Law, the law that is superior to what purports to be the law of the state—demanded. An act could, therefore, appear to be an act of civil disobedience while in reality it was an act of obedience—disobedience of a lower law, which was in fact no law at all when tested against the Higher Law, like a statute, ordinance, or court judgment that is without legal force because it is unconstitutional.

This halakhic view leaves nothing beyond reach of the Rule of Law. It does not open the door to the claims of the individual's subjective conscience. On the other hand, this view incorporates into the Rule of Law itself the weightiest claims of the conscience and poses a problem for the individual when demands are made to commit murder, or grossly immoral acts, or acts that the religious conscience would consider idolatrous.

This resolution of the possibilities inherent in a confrontation between law and conscience could be effected only in a social order in which theoretically there was no distinction between law and religion, between religion and conscience, between conscience and law. In such an order, the law could be looked to for answers to *all* questions.

This all-inclusive legal order comprehended within itself certain laws, which could be peculiarly denominated as *laws* of conscience, or natural *laws*—the *laws* that God had "revealed" to the sons of Noah—*laws* that were applicable to all men and women everywhere, whether Greek or Jew, barbarian, Scythian, bond, or free.[25] But again, these laws were not outside the legal order. They may confront the human being but they do not confront, as outside challengers, the legal order.

Biblical Hebrew had no word for conscience.[26] This does not mean that what we call conscience played no role in the Hebrew Scriptures or in post-Biblical Jewish thought. In Jewish thought it was assumed that the heart could tell a person that he is guilty or innocent. Job says, "I hold fast my righteousness, and will not let it go; my heart does not reproach me for any of my days."[27] In I Samuel the incident is related of David cutting off the skirt of Saul's robe and is then followed with this comment: "And afterward David's heart smote him, because he had cut off Saul's skirt."[28] As Werblowsky has noted,

> the Talmudic language of the rabbis, who were quite familiar with pangs of conscience and scruples, still speaks only of the "beating" or "palpitating" heart, and even Bahya ibn Pakuda (Spain, eleventh century), one of the most outstanding representatives of the ascetic spirituality that blossomed under the influence of Neoplatonism and Sufism, calls his beautiful and widely read work "The Book of the Duties of the Heart."[29]

But if one is going to speak of the "duties of the *heart*," it must become obvious that *everyone* has a heart. Whether one has stood at the foot of Sinai or not, one is bound by the duties imposed on the "sons of Noah." There is a pre-existent law that provides a content for the heart (or conscience). Each man has a heart, but each man is not a law unto himself. The heart or conscience is not a voice that speaks *out* of man; it is a hearing agency given to man so that he may *hear* the voice of God.

Today, when extreme forms of individualism often play a dominant role in religious or moral thought, conscience is often thought to have a legislative function; it makes the law *for*, yet *in*, the individual, a law which cannot be violated if one is to be true to oneself; and being true to oneself seems to be the fundamental precept of the moral order.

This is remote, indeed, from the traditional Jewish position. The heart or conscience has a reporting but not an originating function. It does not make law but only tells a man whether or not he has violated the law which transcends his person and life and which makes demands on him. The law calls to the person; the call is heard in and by the heart; but it is not the voice of man that is heard but the voice of God or of the law. Man is true to himself only by being true to the law.

V

In his treatise on the Decalogue, Philo of Alexandria discusses oaths in which the name of God may be invoked. The oath, he says, is an appeal to God as a witness on a matter in dispute. Would a man ask his friend to bear false witness for him? What would the friend think of such a request? But the perjuror does just this: he dares to call on God to bear false witness for him. Moreover, says Philo, look into the heart of the perjuror, and what will you find there?

> You will see there a mind not at peace but full of uproar and confusion, labouring under accusation, suffering all manner of insult and reviling [i.e., self-inflicted wounds]. For every soul has for its birth-fellow and house-mate a monitor whose way is to admit nothing that calls for censure, whose nature is ever to hate evil and love virtue, who is its accuser and its judge in one. . . . Can it be, then, that on a matter on which you would not dare to cite even a friend you do not blush to call God to witness, God the Father and Ruler of the World? . . . But if you are convinced of His providence as a certainty, there is no further height of impiety which remains for you to reach when you say to God, if not with your mouth and tongue, at any rate with your conscience, "Witness to a falsehood for me, share my evil-doing and knavery. The one hope I have of maintaining my good name with men is that Thou shouldest disguise the truth. Be wicked for the sake of another, the superior for the sake of the inferior, the Divine, the best of all, for a man, and a bad man to boot."[30]

The entire passage makes sense only on the supposition that the perjuror has no power to make his own law; that he is subject to a law and a Legislator that are beyond his power to manipulate. But what the perjuror tries to do is to subvert the ordained order, to make the law of God subordinate to the will of a man—"and a bad man to boot."

In the Hellenistic writings, the Greek term *Syneidesis* and the Latin *conscientia* were used for what we would today speak of as conscience. One or the other term was used by Philo, Plutarch, and Seneca, among many others.[31] "It is clear," it has been noted,

> that *conscience* only came into its own in the Greek world after the collapse of the city-state. The close integration of politics with ethics, with the former predominant, was no longer possible: there was no sufficiently close authority, external to the individual, effectively to direct conduct. Consequently, as a *pis aller*, men fell back on the internal chastisement of *conscience* as the only authority.[32]

For the Jew, however, even as the passage from Philo makes clear, the Torah remained "the only authority." Even if he substituted "conscience" for "heart," he still meant that the content of his morality was the God-given law.

Against this background it becomes easier than would otherwise be the case to understand Paul's use of "conscience" in his letter to the church that he had founded in Corinth and whose members, together with their founder and guide, had been Jews. There was strife among them. How should they resolve their differences? To what authority could they look for answers to the questions that perplexed them? For example, they had among them a member who was living with his stepmother. Was such conduct "lawful" for a member of the Christian church, and, if not, how should his fellow Christians treat him?[33] The Jewish law explicitly prohibited a man from living with his father's wife.[34] "Let him who has done this be removed from among you," Paul wrote. "Drive out the wicked person from among you."[35] Paul follows this decision, which he handed down with the authority of a rabbi (which he had been trained to be), with a general instruction:

Do you not know that the unrighteous will not inherit the kingdom of God? Do not be deceived; neither the immoral, nor idolators, nor adulterers, nor homosexuals, nor thieves, nor the greedy, nor drunkards, nor revilers, nor robbers will inherit the kingdom of God. . . . "All things are lawful for me," but not all things are helpful. "All things are lawful for me," but I will not be enslaved by anything. . . . Shun immorality.[36]

Paul's moral instruction to the Corinthians is not essentially different from the rabbinic teaching with regard to the Seven Laws, a body of universal natural law that was given to the sons of Noah. In essence, what Paul said to his congregation was that all things had not become lawful for them; that Christians, Jews, pagans—all men and women everywhere—were bound by the laws revealed to the sons of Noah, who had become, after the Flood, the progenitors of the human race. Ultimate serious questions of morality are not left to be answered by each man according to his own conscience, his own heart, his own subjective will. Liberty, says Paul, is not license; for license means enslavement to one's willfulness, to the lusts of the body.

Thus Paul, when he withdrew from Judaism, took with him into the Christian church the rabbinic conception of a natural law, a natural morality, the conception of a Higher Law, which imposed restraints and limits on governments and men. In fact, all things are *not* lawful. Paul was accustomed to speak in paradoxes; he could state contradictions with remarkable unawareness and innocence. "Paul could be brilliantly inconsistent," it has been noted; "he does not furnish a systematic theology but throws out flashes of insight." He was, after all, a Jew—"The Hebrew mind could hold opposites together and state each side of the truth without seeing any inconsistency."[37]

But it is not only from the teachings of Judaism that Paul could have derived the concept of conscience. The idea had entered the Hellenistic world after the collapse of the city-state, which happened centuries before the rise of Christianity. By the time of Paul the idea had become commonplace.[38] To cite only two examples, Plutarch, who was Paul's contemporary, said that conscience was "like an ulcer in the flesh. It implants in the soul a remorse which never ceases to wound and goad it. Any other pain can be reasoned away, but this remorse is inflicted by reason, on the soul which is so racked with shame, and self-chastised."[39] And Seneca, another of Paul's contemporaries, wrote that it is foolish to pray for a sound understanding.

There is no need to raise our hands to heaven: there is no need to implore the temple warden to allow us close to the ear of some graven image, as though this increased the chances of our being heard. God is near you, is with you, is inside you. Yes, Lucilius, there resides within us a divine spirit, which guards us and watches us in the evil and good we do. . . . In each and every good man "A god (what god we are uncertain) dwells."[40]

In his letter to the Roman church, Paul neatly fuses the lines of thought from the Jewish tradition and Greek ideas. Jews, he writes, will be acceptable to God as they are judged on their merits. The test for them will be, not knowledge of the law, but the extent to which they obeyed its precepts. But Gentiles, too, who do not have the law, will be judged on their merits. For each of them has a conscience, a heart; they know the difference between good and evil. Being outside the law does not mean that they are left without a moral guide:

Therefore, you have no excuse, O man, whoever you are. . . . For He will render to every man according to his works. . . . There will be tribulation and distress for every human being who does evil, the Jew first and also the Greek, but glory and honor and peace for everyone who does good, the Jew first and also the Greek. For God shows no partiality. . . .

When Gentiles who have not the law do by nature what the law requires, they are a law to themselves, even though they do not have the law. They show that what the law requires is written on their hearts, while their conscience also bears witness.[41]

But suppose the conscience misleads? Suppose that the conscience or heart finds nothing wrong with a man living with his stepmother? Apparently, Paul could not conceive of such a case, for he assumed that there was a body of moral precepts that was known to the hearts of both Jews and Gentiles, and when one of the precepts or moral laws was violated, the heart or conscience condemned the act. "It is actually reported," he wrote to Corinth, "that there is immorality among you, and of a kind that is not found even among pagans. . . . Let him who has done this be removed from among you."[42]

In his letter to the Roman Christians, Paul writes that the evildoers, whether they be Jews or Greeks, are "without excuse." "For what can be known about God is plain to them, because God has shown it to them."

What evil acts or habits does Paul condemn? After a special condemnation of men and women who engaged in unnatural sexual relations, Paul condemns those who do things for which they deserve to die: "They were filled with all manner of wickedness, evil, covetousness, malice. Full of envy, murder, strife, deceit, malignity, they are gossips. Slanderers, haters of God, insolent, haughty, boastful, inventors of evil, disobedient to parents, foolish, faithless, heartless, ruthless."[43] No one, Jew or pagan, could be heard to say that his heart approved such acts, that his conscience did not condemn such acts as evil. There was an order of binding values which no one was free to violate on the claim that he hears a different drumbeat, for he must lie or be in grave error if, pursuing evil, he claims that his conscience is clear.[44]

Scholars seem to agree that the pagan use of *syneidesis* or *conscientia* was consistently negative or judicial; that is, the conscience passed judgment on an act that had already been committed. An evil deed evoked a bad or guilty conscience.[45] There is a difference of opinion, however, whether Paul's usage of the term was entirely consistent with the pagan usage. Pierce, for example, says, "But *conscience* in Greek, and the N.T. . . . does not look to the future; its reference is to acts at least begun, if not irrevocably completed, in the past. It tells me that what I have done is sin."[46] According to Father D'Arcy, however, St. Paul should be given credit for certain innovations with respect to conscience. The term occurs twenty-three times in Paul's epistles, and in fifteen of these it has the meaning that the term had for pagan writers—that it was retrospective in its direction and judicial in its function. In eight instances, however, two new features may be found, namely, that the conscience may be subject to error, and that the conscience purports to legislate, to direct prospective action.[47]

St. Paul, then, introduces an entirely new phase in the history of the term "conscience" in moral theory, and two new features characterize his use of it. First, it is to play a *directive* role *before* action takes place. In the pagan writers conscience did not appear on the scene until *after* the action was performed, and its role was purely *judicial*; but in St. Paul, conscience is credited with a legislative function, and it induces an obligation in the proper sense. Second, conscience is fallible: the directions it issues may be mistaken; but whether it be mistaken or not, it seems that we are bound to follow its rulings.[48]

This is, I believe, making an excessive claim for St. Paul. For whatever the words they used, pagan philosophers often spoke as if they believed that the conscience can order a person not to undertake a course of action *before* that person has started on its course; that the conscience issues "cease and desist" orders before a person has done anything evil except in contemplation. Plato's *Apology* readily comes to mind in this connection. If he should be acquitted, Socrates said, on condition that in the future he would lead a different kind of life than the kind which had gotten him into his desperate situation, his response would be as follows:

"Men of Athens, I respect and love you, but I shall obey the god rather than you, and while I live and am able to continue, I shall never give up philosophy or stop exhorting you and pointing out the truth to any one of you whom I may meet. . . ." For know that the god commands me to do this. . . . Therefore I say to you, men of Athens, either do as Anytus tells you, or not, and either acquit me, or not, knowing that I shall not change my conduct even if I am to die many times over.[49]

Socrates related the incident when the Thirty tried to involve him in a criminal action that would have led to the execution of Leon of Salamis: "Then I, however, showed again, by action, not in word only, that I did not care a whit for death if that be not too rude an expression, but that I did care with all my might not to do anything unjust or unholy. For that government [of the Thirty], with all its power, did not frighten me into doing anything unjust."[50] Conscience, in these instances, worked prospectively, legislatively, to prevent Socrates from entering upon an evil course of conduct. Clearly, in these cases, conscience did not act to condemn, to pass judgment upon an evil act already done or commenced.

It is to be noted, however, that Socrates speaks of the voice within him as having a negative effect, as commanding him not to do a certain act: "Something divine and spiritual comes to me, the very thing which Meletus ridiculed in his indictment. I have had this from my childhood; it is a sort of voice that comes to me, and when it comes it always holds me back from what I am thinking of doing, but never urges me forward."[51] Indeed, Socrates himself referred to this voice within him as having a future thrust, rather than something that condemned only past actions:

> For hitherto the customary prophetic monitor always spoke to me very frequently and opposed me even in very small matters, if I was going to do anything I should not; . . . but the divine sign did not oppose me either when I left my home in the morning, or when I came here to the court, or at any point of my speech, when I was going to say anything; and yet on other occasions it stopped me at many points in the midst of a speech.[52]

Or take as one other example, Epictetus, who was a contemporary of St. Paul and Plutarch. I submit that in the following passages, selected almost at random, it is impossible to find a basis for a distinction between the prospective and retrospective functions of the conscience:

·I must die: must I, then, die groaning too? I must be fettered: and wailing too? I must go into exile: does anyone, then, keep me from going with a smile and cheerful and serene? "Tell your secrets." I say not a word: for this is under my control. "But I will fetter you." What is that you say, man? fetter *me*? My leg you will fetter, but my moral purpose not even Zeus himself has power to overcome. "I will throw you into prison." My paltry body, rather! "I will behead you." Well, when did I ever tell you that mine was the only neck that could not be severed?[53]

This passage, as well as the next one to be quoted, means at least this: that no human power can force a good person to do an evil act. The individual may be threatened with imprisonment, with exile, even with death, but he will not do what his conscience would condemn. There is nothing retrospective in this view of conscience. The good person does not feel remorse or guilt, for he has avoided that which would taint him.

In a later passage Epictetus again considers the threats that may be hurled at the good man—poverty, loss of office, exile, and even death:

Is it for this that the tyrant inspires fear? Is it because of this that his guards seem to have long and sharp swords? Let others see to that; I have considered all this, no one has authority over me. I have been set free by God, I know His commands, no one has power any longer to make a slave of me. . . . Again I yield up to you all these things [my body, my property, my home] and my whole paltry body itself, whenever you will. Do make trial of your power, and you will find out how far it extends. . . . I regard God's will as better than my will. I shall attach myself to Him as a servant and follower, my choice is one with His, my desire one with His, in a word, my will is one with His will.[54]

Whether Socrates or Plato or the Stoics used a word, Greek or Latin, meaning conscience is not important in the history of the idea, though it may be important to the lexicographer. And I think that an unprejudiced reading of the relevant texts shows that to these philosophers the conscience spoke legislatively and prospectively, and it was precisely because it performed this function that conscience was of such transcendent importance. The retrospective, judicial use of the conscience cannot compare in importance, precisely because this function of the conscience is identified with the past, with what has been done and cannot be undone. It is the difference between planning the future and brooding over the past.

And if we look again at the incidents from the Hebrew Scriptures which we considered at the beginning of this essay, it will be seen that, in the incidents recorded, conscience played a legislative rather than a judicial role. The "Hebrew midwives," because they feared God, did not act as the king had commanded them, "but saved the men-children alive"; and so, too, the servants of King Saul—his guardsmen—refused to obey his order to murder the priests; and so, too, Daniel, despite the king's decree, continued to pray to God. And so, too, the various books of Maccabees record numerous incidents of Jews welcoming martyrdom rather than allowing themselves to perform acts which they considered abominations. The struggle of the Jews to frustrate the intent of Caligula to violate the sanctity of the Temple was related by Josephus in clear terms of the prospective force of conscience. The Jews, prepared for martyrdom, put Petronius on notice that if he will not disobey Caesar, they will not disobey God.

Paul Tillich gives a different interpretation, according to which the demanding, prospective conscience—the warning conscience—is only the anticipation of the judging or condemning conscience. He says, in *The Protestant Era*:

The fact that self and conscience are dependent on the experience of personal guilt explains the prevalance of the "bad conscience" in reality, literature, and theory. It gives evidence of the assertion that the uneasy, accusing, and judging conscience is the original phenomenon; that the good conscience is only the absence of the bad conscience; and that the demanding and warning conscience is only the anticipation of it. Since ego-self and conscience grow in mutual dependence and since the self discovers itself in the experience of a split between what it is and what it ought to be, the basic character of the conscience—the consciousness of guilt—is obvious.[55]

This view is based on the theory that self-consciousness arises out of a sense of guilt, which is conscience. Without this sense of guilt, or conscience, there would be no awareness of the "inner man," of selfhood.

One may accept the notion that consciousness of self is rooted in consciousness of guilt, or conscience, without necessarily concluding that this sense of guilt is primarily of a retrospective character. We are called upon to act and to anticipate just as we are called upon to recall our past actions; perhaps we must chart our future course even before we reflect upon our past course of actions, to legislate for ourselves even before we judge ourselves. Of course, legislation is an anticipation of future judgment, which says, "If you do this act, such and such will happen; if you do this act, you will be sorry!" But it also says categorically, "Thou shalt do this!" It makes positive as well as negative commandments. True enough that the positive commandment can easily be translated into a negative one. "Feed the hungry" can be made to read "Do not deny food to the hungry," and the negative commandment can be put in conditional form, "If you deny food to the hungry, then such and such may follow, and you will be sorry," or simply, "If you do not do what is right, your conscience will trouble you, it will give you no rest."

But it seems to me that these translations falsify the subjective facts. The Hebrew midwives or Saul's guards were not sophisticated persons. They simply heard the voice of conscience say that they must not murder innocent persons, even when ordered to do so by the king of Egypt or the king of Israel. It is forcing things, I think, to say that these people at the moment of decision thought that if they obeyed the command to kill, their consciences would trouble them ever after; for perhaps their consciences would trouble them if they did *not* kill, for disobedience of the king's order would bring in its train heaps of trouble, of the most horrible kinds, upon themselves, their families, and friends. One might argue further that especially sophisticated persons—for example, Socrates when he refused to bargain with the jury or when he refused to break loose from jail, or Thomas More when he persisted in his refusal to save his life by the utterance of a few words—would not be prone to translate a demanding conscience into an anticipatory accusing, judging conscience. For they saw themselves as servants of God, and not of the jury or the king, as hearing the unconditional law of God and not of the state, as standing before their Ruler and Judge now and eternally.

VI

Since in classical Judaism the law is conceived as being all-embracive, covering all contingencies, and incorporating the basic and indispensable principles of natural law or morality, almost no room was left for the individual's subjective conscience. As seen in normative Judaism, King Saul's guardsmen, the martyrs of the books of Maccabees, the Jews who confronted Petronius, Daniel, or even the "Hebrew midwives," did not need to plead conscience; they could have pointed to the Noachide or halakhic laws as the basis for their actions.[56] Whatever the question, whatever the problem, the answer could be found in the objective law.[57]

This is not to say, as we have seen, that conscience was unknown to Judaism. But the genius of Judaism was to translate the dictates or work of conscience into legal principles; and in theory nothing important was left beyond the pale of the law; all that was conceivably important in conscience had been assimilated into the law—as English equity law assimilated moral principles.

Christianity, however, with its strong antinomian bias, took a different course. The early church, as the Epistles of St. Paul show, had to face the challenges that came from Jewish converts who still had ties to halakhic principles and practices, and from pagan converts whose lives and actions tended to reflect Roman or other customs or systems of secular law. On what could the Christian fall back in a crisis except the imperative claims of his conscience?

But of course one's conscience is fallible. It may not condemn one, when it should; or it may misdirect one. Scholastic philosophers were aware of these problems.[58] Many medieval moralists took a position against the claims of conscience by arguing, on the strength of a point made by St. Augustine, that a subordinate authority is not binding if it runs counter to the command of a superior authority, "as for instance, if the proconsul were to enjoin what the Emperor forbade."[59] But what if the proconsul appears to speak in the name of the Emperor— if the subordinate authority (the conscience) claims to speak at the command of the superior authority (God)? St. Albert the Great, in the thirteenth century, took the position that conscience, or the subjective factor, must be controlling and must be recognized as having sovereign authority.[60]

The position taken by Albert became the position of St. Thomas Aquinas and appears to be that of Catholic theologians generally. It has been summarized as follows: "If conscience, rightly or wrongly, declares an action to be commanded by God, and a man decides to do the opposite, he cannot avoid sin. The reason he [St. Thomas] gives is simple, and it seems to be decisive: 'As far as lies within him, a man [who has heard the voice of conscience but chooses to disobey it] is determined not to obey the will of God.'"[61] The conscience may be in error, and the error should be removed and the judgment of conscience should be reversed; but as long as the judgment of conscience stands, a person is bound not to act against it.[62] Any other answer would mean that a person may consciously choose to disobey what he believes to be the judgment of God. To one who identifies the voice of conscience with the voice of God, there can be no alternative; he is bound not to act against his conscience. With Martin Luther he can only say: "*Ich kann nicht anders!*"

St. Thomas contended that to despise the command of conscience, if one believes that conscience is the voice of God, is the same thing as to despise the command of God. Contemporary Catholic teaching takes the argument to the positive conclusion "that it is the same thing to obey the command of conscience as to obey the command of God."[63]

Since in a specific situation the conscience may fall into error, the church found it necessary to intervene, to assert its authority, to make its priests advisers and guides; and for the instruction of priests, casuistry—the science of dealing with cases of conscience—developed.

It may be, as Tillich contends, that for Thomas Aquinas and the Catholic church generally, as well as for Luther, the authority of the conscience was limited to the ethical sphere, and that they did not recognize the possibility of a religious conscience; thus there could not be a heresy avowed with a good conscience: heresy had to be seen as simply a demonic possession and condemned as being, perhaps literally, the work of the devil.[64] I think that this may be an overrefinement that falsifies the subjective facts. Surely the early Christian martyrs—like the Maccabees before them and like the Jews who offered their lives in defense of the Temple against the threats of Caligula— would not have recognized this limitation on conscience, or the sharp separation of religion from morals, and it is doubtful if traditional Catholics—or Puritan Calvinists—could have made this separation.

In any case, after Calvin we see the proliferation of religious sects, and religious enthusiasts claiming conscience as the source of their religious insights, and we find in due course the recognition of the fact of religious pluralism, and the wisdom of religious toleration as the state's policy. Religious conscience comes of age with the Reformation sectarian movements.

In considering Calvin in this context, it is important to note the great difference between the tone and direction of the *Institutes of a Christian Religion*, written in their final version in 1559, and his subsequent Biblical commentaries, especially the *Commentaries on the Book of the Prophet Daniel*, written in 1561. As the late George H. Sabine noted:

> In its initial form Calvinism not only included a condemnation of resistance but it lacked all leaning toward liberalism, constitutionalism, or representative principles. Where it had free range it developed characteristically into a theocracy, a kind of oligarchy maintained by an alliance of the clergy and the gentry from which the mass of the people was excluded and which was, in general, illiberal, oppressive, and reactionary.... In practice, wherever possible, Calvinist government [as in Geneva and Massachusetts] placed the two swords of Christian tradition in the church, and gave the direction of secular authority to the clergy rather than to secular rulers. The result was likely to be an intolerable rule of the saints: a meticulous regulation of the most private concerns founded upon universal espionage, with only a shadowy distinction between the maintenance of public order, the control of private morals, and the preservation of pure doctrine and worship.[65]

As long as Calvin had power in Geneva and could hope that his form of Protestantism would become the religion of the French kings, he, like Luther, stressed the divine right of the secular power and the duty of passive obedience. It is, he wrote, "impossible to resist the magistrate without, at the same time, resisting God himself."[66] Kings have, of course, duties to their subjects; God's law is binding on the ruler no less than on those ruled by him; but the evil ruler is one "raised by him [God] to punish the iniquity of the people."[67]

> Wherefore, if we are inhumanly harassed by a cruel prince; if we are rapaciously plundered by an avaricious or luxurious one; if we are neglected by an indolent one; or if we are persecuted, on account of piety, by an impious and sacrilegious one, let us first call to mind our

transgressions against God, which he undoubtedly chastises by these scourges. Thus our impatience will be restrained by humility. Let us, in the next place, consider that it is not our province to remedy these evils, and that nothing remains for us, but to implore the aid of the Lord.[68]

While private persons had no right to resist tyranny, Calvin conceded the possibility and propriety of inferior officers deriving from God the right of resistance. He referred to the ephori, who were a check upon the kings of the Lacedaemonians, the plebian tribunes of Rome, and the demarchi, who were a check upon the Athenian senate. Such officers, Calvin wrote, betray the liberties of their people if they fail to oppose the violence or cruelty of kings—"such forbearance involves the most nefarious perfidy."[69] One can see here the need of the idea of constitutional checks and balances, the power of impeachment, and the power of judicial review of legislative and executive action. But these are institutions provided by a constitution; they are not expressions of the private religious or moral conscience.

Calvin, however, in the *Institutes*, recognized one exception to the duty of obedience to government: If the rulers command anything that is against God, "it ought not to have the least attention; nor, in this case, ought we to pay any regard to all that dignity attached to magistrates." At this point Calvin cites the case of Daniel: "On this principle Daniel denied that he had committed any crime against the king in disobeying his impious decree; because the king had exceeded the limits of his office, and had not only done an injury to men, but, by raising his arm against God, had degraded his own authority."[70] In matters pertaining to religion, "We ought to obey God rather than men,"[71] and "suffer anything rather than deviate from piety."

When it became apparent to Calvin that his followers were not going to have an easy time in France, the Netherlands, and elsewhere, he concentrated on his right or duty of resistance when the temporal jurisdiction threatened the spiritual realm.

In his *Commentaries on the Book of the Prophet Daniel*, written some years after the final edition of the *Institutes*, he argued that fear of God must come ahead of honor of kings. To reverse the order would be a perversion of the order of nature, for kings obtain their authority only from the fear of God.

For if anyone begins his reverence of an earthly prince by rejecting that of God, he will act preposterously, since this is a complete perversion of the order of nature. Then let God be feared in the first place, and earthly princes will obtain their authority. . . . Daniel, therefore, . . . defends himself with justice, since *he had not committed any crime against the king*; for he was compelled to obey the command of God, and he neglected what the king had ordered in opposition to it. For earthly princes lay aside all their power when they rise up against God, and are unworthy of being reckoned in the number of mankind. We ought rather utterly to defy them than to obey them whenever they are so restive and wish to spoil God of his rights, and, as it were, to seize upon his throne and draw him down from heaven.[72]

One does not need Christianity, or the Reformation, or the Protestant conscience to understand or interpret the case of Daniel, purportedly a Jew of the sixth century B.C.E. (though the book may have been written in the second century B.C.E.). In its essentials it is not different from the case of the Maccabees and other cases of civil disobedience related in the apocryphal books, or by Philo or Josephus. When Peter said, "We ought to obey God rather than men,"[73] he spoke as a Jew to other Jews, to whom he did not need to explain what he meant by this proposition. We should remember, too, as noted earlier, that it was Socrates who said, to the Athenian jury that tried him: "Men of Athens, I respect and love you, but I shall obey the god rather than you."[74] If Luke was the author of *The Acts of the Apostles*, it is possible that he was familiar with Plato's *Apology*.[75] The author of the book of Daniel, the authors of the apocryphal books, Philo and Josephus, Peter and the apostles, the authors[76] of the New Testament—all lived and participated in Hellenistic Jewry, and all were, more or less, at home in both Jewish thought and Greek culture.[77] Whether they knew the word for it or not, all were familiar with what came to be known as conscience.

Calvin, therefore, broke no new ground in his *Commentaries on the Book of the Prophet Daniel*. His stand on civil disobedience had behind it a well-established Jewish-Christian-Hellenic Hellenistic tradition that insisted on the primacy of the law of God over the pretended law of an earthly ruler, and the duty of the subject to disregard the impious order of the king.

The thrust of the Reformation toward religious liberty owes relatively little to Calvin, at whose door must be placed responsibility for the persecution of Servetus and Castellio. The founders of the Reformation, when and where they gained power, were not reluctant to resort to fire and the sword. They proved that religious fanatics and ideologues are no more to be trusted with power than are totalitarian politicians. Religious toleration was as far removed from their thoughts and spirit as religious persecution was from the thoughts and spirit of Erasmus or Castellio or Bayle. The prophet Daniel had the right to disobey the ungodly order of the king, but he would have had no right to disobey the order of the Town Council of Geneva, which was carrying out the wishes of Calvin, and therefore the wishes of God.

But the Protestant Reformation delivered a great deal more than was expressly promised by Calvin and the other Reformation leaders. Once the church and its priests were eliminated as mediators of the individual's conscience, and casuistry was discountenanced, and the Bible became subject to an open-ended variety of interpretations, and a church was seen as a voluntary congregation or association of men and women, the individual conscience received a divine or religious sanction. Given the mixture of ingredients, no other result was possible. Its roots, as we have seen, are deeply planted in the Hebrew Scriptures and Jewish history, in Christian martyrology, in the life and death of Socrates, in Hellenistic culture; but its flowering came only with the Protestant Reformation, which, almost unknowingly, took into itself this rich heritage, together with some elements from the Renaissance, and gave the world what may be gratefully acknowledged as the Protestant conscience.

Whether individualism could have developed without the idea of the individual conscience, or whether the individual conscience could have developed without the idea of individualism, is a matter of speculation, but I believe that a strong case can be made for the priority of the individual conscience, for the proposition that the roots of the idea of individualism are to be found in religious thought.[78] In any case, we find the ideas intertwined, and perhaps inseparable. In the modern period of history, the religious conscience seems to have asserted itself before the moral conscience gained recognition.

VII

Religious toleration is not the product only of a belief in the rights of religious conscience. Religious toleration may be based in part on the value of civil peace—freedom of a community from civil strife—and the interest in sincerity of religious piety. In the *Tractatus Theologico-Politicus*, Spinoza stated the case in these words:

> Seeing that we have the rare happiness of living in a republic, where everyone's judgment is free and unshackled, and where each may worship God as his conscience dictates, and where freedom is esteemed before all things dear and precious, I have believed that I should be undertaking no ungrateful or unprofitable task, in demonstrating that not only can such freedom be granted without prejudice to the public peace, but also, that without such freedom, piety cannot flourish, nor the public peace be secured.[79]

Spinoza's arguments for religious toleration were published in 1670. In 1689 there was published Locke's *Letter Concern-*

ing Toleration,[80] which became one of the most influential pleas
for a free church in a free society. Although no innovator—
toleration had been advocated by Independents and others for
years[81]—Locke's *Letter* won attention perhaps because of its
strong emphasis on principles, while not neglecting prudential
arguments. Like his *Second Treatise on Civil Government*,
Locke's *Letter Concerning Toleration* attempted a theoretical
formulation of rational grounds. Because of the principled line
it took, Locke's work had the effect of underscoring the legiti-
macy and force of the religious conscience.

At the very beginning of the *Letter* Locke takes a stand on
the side of conscience. Christianity, he says, is a religion of the
heart. One usurps the name of Christian only if one is "without
holiness of life, purity of manners, benignity and meekness of
spirit." These qualities of character can be achieved only by
love—not by force. Persecution on account of religion will not
lead to the honest adoption of Christianity. Where there is conversion without reformation, there is, in truth, no conversion.
One should, therefore, begin with oneself and not with one's
neighbor. One must oneself depart from immorality and vice,
destroy their roots in oneself before one undertakes to extirpate
sects one does not like. In making this argument, Locke says
that he appeals to the "consciences of those that persecute,
torment, destroy, and kill other men upon pretense of religion."[82] A man who has himself achieved the character of a true
Christian would not ever go about armed with the sword but
only with the Gospel of peace. Toleration in matters of religion
is so "agreeable" to the Gospel of Jesus and "to the genuine
reason of mankind" that it is "monstrous"—and "altogether in-
credible"—that men should be so blind as not to see "the necessity and advantage" of a policy of toleration.

Locke's case for a policy of religious toleration is set forth in
principled steps:

1. Religion falls outside the interests of civil government. A
commonwealth is "a society of men constituted only for procur-

ing, preserving, and advancing their own civil interests." These
interests are "life, liberty, health, and indolency of body; and the
possession of outward things, such as money, lands, houses,
furniture, and the like." It is the duty of government to secure
to all people in the commonwealth "the just possession of these
things belonging to this life." It has no concern "for the interest
of men's souls." Its power cannot be extended to include "the
salvation of souls." The "care of souls" is not committed to the
government nor to "other men." God has not committed to any
individual authority over another's religion, nor can the people
themselves consent to vest such power in the government,
"because no man can so far abandon the care of his own salvation as blindly to leave to the choice of any other, whether
prince or subject, to prescribe to him what faith or worship he
shall embrace."[83]

2. Why cannot power over religion be vested in the government or in another person? The answer to this question points
up an essential quality of religion: "All the life and power of true
religion consists in the inward and full persuasion of the mind;
and faith is not faith without believing." The power of government "consists only in outward force; but true and saving religion consists in the inward persuasion of the mind, without
which nothing can be acceptable to God," and the nature of
mind is such that it cannot be reached by confiscation of property, imprisonment, or torture. Only "light and evidence" can be
effective to change people's minds; penalties are incapable to
produce beliefs. It follows that the government has no power to
establish "any articles of faith, or forms of worship," by force of
law.[84]

3. If power over religion were vested in government, people
would need to abdicate their reason and their conscience, and
blindly resign themselves to the will of their government and
the religion which ignorance, ambition, or superstition may
have chanced to establish in their native country. But in fact for
every person there may be one religion that may be the true one,

and therefore but one country may be in the right while all the rest of the world may be obliged to follow a variety of paths to destruction. It hardly conforms to one's notion of the Deity to suppose that people should owe their eternal happiness or misery to the accident of where they happened to have been born.[85]

4. Just as one's religion should not depend on where one was born, so too, it should not depend on the church into which one was born. "Nobody is born a member of any church." A church is "a free and voluntary society." It is utterly absurd to think that we inherit the religion of our parents—to view religion in the same way as we view property and estates. "No man by nature is bound unto any particular church or sect, but everyone joins himself voluntarily to that society in which he believes he has found that profession and worship which is truly acceptable to God." One should enter a religious communion, and remain there, only as long as it satisfies one's hope of salvation, only as long as it provides one with the bonds that proceed from "the certain expectation of eternal life." "A church, then, is a society of members voluntarily uniting to that end."[86]

5. Since a church is a strictly voluntary society, organized and maintained for a limited purpose, it alone may make rules for its self-governance. These rules may include provisions for dealing with members who are recalcitrant. A church may resort to exhortation, admonition, and advice, and if these measures do not accomplish their purpose, it may expel the member from its body and refuse thereafter to render that person the services theretofore enjoyed. But there may be no punishment or prejudice beyond these actions.

No private person has any right in any manner to prejudice another person in his civil enjoyments because he is of another church or religion. All his rights and franchises that belong to him as a man, or as a denizen, are inviolably to be preserved to him. These are not the business of religion. No violence nor injury is to be offered him whether he be Christian or Pagan. Nay, we must not content ourselves with narrow measures of bare justice; charity, bounty, and liberality must be added to it. . . . If any man err from the right way, it is his own misfortune, no injury to thee nor therefore art thou to punish him in the things of this life because thou supposest he will be miserable in that which is to come.[87]

And churches should stand in the same relation toward one another as do private persons, without any pretense of superiority or jurisdiction over one another. No church is orthodox; no church is heretical—"For every church is orthodox to itself, to others, erroneous or heretical."[88]

6. A church may be viewed from the standpoint of its articles of faith or of its forms of worship. Both are beyond the authority of government. For both these aspects of a church concern "the salvation of souls," and thus concern in no way the commonwealth. "Neither the use nor the omission of any ceremonies in these religious assemblies does either advantage or prejudice the life, liberty, or estate of any man."[89]

7. But suppose a church should institute infant sacrifices as part of its worship? Of course this practice may be prohibited and punished, because the killing of infants is not lawful in any context. The laws against murder are not made about religious matters; they are not made in order to regulate forms of worship.

But those things that are prejudicial to the commonweal of a people in their ordinary use, and are therefore forbidden by laws, those things ought not to be permitted to churches in their sacred rites. Only the magistrate ought always to be very careful that he do not misuse his authority to the oppression of any church, under pretense of public good.[90]

Articles of faith may not be imposed by law on any church.

For it is absurd that things should be enjoined by laws which are not in men's power to perform. . . . But (will some say) let men at least profess that they believe. A sweet religion, indeed, that obliges men to dissemble and tell lies, both to God and man, for the salvation of their souls![91]

Furthermore, the law may not forbid the preaching or profession of any speculative opinions in any church, because such opinions have no relation to the civil rights of subjects.

> If a Roman Catholic believe that to be really the body of Christ, which another man calls bread, he does no injury thereby to his neighbour. If a Jew do not believe the New Testament to be the word of God, he does not thereby alter anything in men's civil rights. If a heathen doubt of both Testaments, he is not therefore to be punished as a pernicious citizen. The power of the magistrate and the estates of the people may be equally secure whether any man believe these things or no. I readily grant that these opinions are false and absurd. But the business of laws is not to provide for the truth of opinions, but for the safety and security of the commonwealth, and of every particular man's goods and person. For the truth certainly would do well enough if she were once left to shift for herself.[92]

8. Nor should the criminal law be opened up to embrace the punishment of sins. Idolatry is a sin against God, but it may not be made a criminal offense. So, too, other sins, such as covetousness, uncharitableness, and idleness—they may not be made into criminal offenses "because they are not prejudicial to other men's rights, nor do they break the public peace of societies." Even the sin of lying may not be made a crime "but only the injury done unto men's neighbours and to the commonwealth."[93]

9. A conflict between state action and individual conscience is possible in two types of situations. (a) The state acts within the compass of its proper authority in a matter relating to private property, or "for the peace, riches, and public commodities of the whole people," or "for the increase of their inward strength against foreign invasions"; yet the action appears unlawful to the conscience of a private person. This, says Locke, "will seldom happen." But assuming that it does, then "I say, that such a person is to abstain from the action that he judges unlawful, and he is to undergo the punishment which it is not unlawful for him to bear. For the private judgment of any person con-

cerning a law enacted in political matters, for the public good, does not take away the obligation of that law, nor deserve a dispensation."[94] (b) The state acts with respect to a matter that lies outside its legitimate authority and that touches upon matters affecting the care of a person's "own eternal happiness"— Locke comments that

> men are not in these days obliged by that law, against their consciences. For the political society is instituted for no other end, but only to secure every man's possession of the things of this life. The care of each man's soul, and of the things of heaven, which neither does belong to the commonwealth nor can be subjected to it, is left entirely to every man's self.[95]

In such a case, it is "evident what liberty remains to men in reference to their eternal salvation, and that is, that every one should do what he in his conscience is persuaded to be acceptable to the Almighty, on whose good pleasure and acceptance depends their eternal happiness. For obedience is due, in the first place, to God, and afterwards to the laws."[96] Such a law was not authorized by anything in the Constitution, nor was the right to enact such a law ever "in the power of the people to grant." What should the individual do? "I answer: The principal and chief care of every one ought to be of his own soul first, and, in the next place, of the public peace."[97]

10. But there are some exceptions to the principle of toleration. (a) Churches may not teach as doctrines of religion any opinions that "manifestly undermine the foundations of society." (b) Churches may not teach that faith is not to be kept with heretics, that an excommunicated king forfeits his crown. A church may not, openly or covertly, "upon pretence of religion," claim that it alone may determine who has lawful authority, for thereby it shows its lack of tolerance of all other churches and all other people.

> I say these have no right to be tolerated by the magistrate; as neither those that will not own and teach the duty of tolerating all men in matters of mere religion. For what do all these and the like doctrines

signify, but that they may, and are ready upon any occasion to seize the government . . . and that they only ask leave to be tolerated by the magistrate so long until they find themselves strong enough to effect it [i.e., its subversion]?[98]

(c) A church has no claim upon the state's toleration if it is founded on the principle that its members owe primary allegiance to a foreign prince. (Locke cited the Muslim religion as an example, but it has been generally recognized that he meant the Roman Catholic Church.) (d) Atheists have no claim on toleration. For "the taking away of God, though but even in thought, dissolves all; besides also, those that by their atheism undermine and destroy all religion, can have no pretence of religion whereupon to challenge the privilege of a toleration."[99]

VIII

Although Locke's *Letter* was by no means the first statement in favor of complete religious toleration (*Concerning Heretics and Those Who Burn Them*, by Balthasar Hubmaier, written in 1524, deserves recognition as probably the first such statement[100]), it calls for special attention because it is generally recognized as the classic statement or plea in favor of a policy of religious toleration. Locke stated principles which, for rational and historical reasons, continue to be the essential and necessary foundation for the rights of conscience and religious liberty. The fundamental principles, abstracted from our discussion above, are, I think, the following:

1. Even though a religion may exclude no action as essentially profane, the civil order must make a distinction between religion and state. Religious interests and actions must be excluded from the state's authority. A church may excommunicate a member or declare that person a heretic, but the church may not turn to the state for the execution of its orders and sanctions, and the religious body itself may not touch the life,

liberty, or property of the person whom it seeks to discipline or whom it expels.

2. From the standpoint of the state, church membership is voluntary. A religious body may claim a person's membership from the date of birth, but no such membership can be imposed on an adult against that person's wishes. Whatever may be the claim of the religious order, the state cannot recognize compulsory church membership.

Given these two principles, a large measure of religious toleration is assured. That does not solve all problems. There is, for example, the vexing question, When is an action purely religious—hence protected against interference by the state? [101] Principles generate problems, but without principles, we would have many more problems, and of staggering proportions. Given the principle of separation of church and state,[102] and the principle of religious voluntarism, the problems left for resolution cannot be of an earth-shaking character. No Hubmaier is martyred by Catholics, no Servetus is burned alive by Calvinists, no Thomas Münzer is executed by Lutherans; there are no religious wars, and no insurmountable obstacles are placed in the way of the development of religious pluralism, religious preaching, and proselytism.

Locke's formulation of the principle of religious toleration, despite its appearance to the contrary, is absolute in its reach. The limits on it are *de facto* and external. Suppose, he says, as we have noted, a church should institute infant sacrifice as part of its worship, would such a killing not be murder? Of course it would be, and punishment of the killer would not be a violation of the principle of religious liberty, *for the laws against murder have not been enacted in order to control or regulate religious matters*. The laws against murder make the killing of persons criminal in *any* context. Their objective is a purely secular one; they are not enacted in order to regulate religious worship. Acts which are forbidden by the general laws are not permitted to churches or religious persons as exceptions. To ask for an exception to the general law is to cross over the line of distinction between church and state.

This Lockean principle has become one of the fundamental tests of constitutionality of legislation as it impinges on religious action: *Does the legislation have a secular purpose?* This is the first constitutional hurdle that a challenged statute must meet. If it fails this test, it is a violation of the First Amendment.[103]

The other limitations to religious toleration noted by Locke are also not really exceptions to the principle. Their exclusion from protection is grounded on secular, not religious, considerations. Certain teachings by churches may be detrimental to or subversive of the social order; they tend to "manifestly undermine the foundations of society." The state may have laws that punish subversive teachings, no matter where or under whatever pretenses they may be taught. The purpose of the legislation is purely secular. Even the exclusion of atheists from toleration is justified by Locke in secular terms: "The taking away of God, though but even in thought, dissolves all"; that is, atheism removes an element without which no social contract can be expected to endure; for conscience must be religious or it is not conscience at all. "Those are not at all to be tolerated who deny the being of a God. Promises, covenants, and oaths, which are the bonds of human society, can have no hold upon an atheist."[104]

It is interesting to note that in a work published almost simultaneously with Locke's *Letter*, Pierre Bayle contended that immoral and antisocial opinions should be punished as criminal acts, but not as heresies; they should be punished simply on the ground that the conduct such views inspired might threaten the security of the community. With respect to atheism, however, Bayle took a position that was more moderate than Locke's: the atheist should be tolerated but may be forbidden to proselytize that opinion.[105]

It may well be that both Bayle and Locke had learned much from Thomas More's *Utopia*, published in 1516 well over a century and a half before Bayle's treatise and Locke's monograph. When a convert to a new religion preached publicly "with more zeal than discretion" and abused those who would not follow him, the Utopians convicted him, "not for despising their religion but for stirring up a riot among the people." It was an ancient principle among them that "no one should suffer for his religion." There was liberty of preaching in Utopia; it was ordained "that it should be lawful for every man to follow the religion of his choice, that each might strive to bring others over to his own, provided that he quietly and modestly supported his own by reasons nor bitterly demolished all others if his persuasions were not successful nor used any violence and refrained from abuse."[106] It was believed that "this method of settlement was in the interest of religion itself." The Utopian lawgiver "was uncertain whether God did not desire a varied and manifold worship and therefore did not inspire different people with different views." The only requirement was that one should handle one's religious views in public "reasonably and moderately"; and this requirement was obviously based on secular and not religious considerations.

But one exception was made in Utopian law: a person who did not believe in immortality and providence was considered to be of sluggish and low disposition, for he reduced man to the level of a beast and thus reduced the dignity of human nature. Such a person was not to be entrusted with public office, nor was he allowed to argue his opinion in public—"But they do not punish him in any way, being convinced that it is in no man's power to believe what he chooses."[107]

In their basic approach to the question of religious dissidence, Erasmus and Thomas More, who were contemporaries and close friends, were in substantial agreement (More, at least insofar as the views expressed in *Utopia* may be taken as the views of its author;[108] and Erasmus contended against persecution of heretics; heresy itself cannot be made a crime. In a letter to George of Saxony he wrote: "It is not right that any error should be punished by fire, unless sedition is added to it, or some other crime that the laws punish by death.")[109] The position of Erasmus has been well summarized as follows:

Whenever Erasmus refers to the dangers of heresy, one may safely read for heresy not mere error in belief, but obstinate and aggressive error, expressed in open revolt against the established church or state, and threatening the peace and unity of the Christian republic. Indeed, in such references heresy is almost always coupled with sedition and schism. The Donatists, as murderers, rebels and schismatics, he considered the worst type of heretics, and most meriting suppression by the state. He cited them repeatedly in his arguments, in one place adding the illuminating comment: "But against the Pelagians there was never any suggestion of an appeal to the power of Caesar, because they did not in the same way disturb the tranquility of the state.". . . From his various comments on the subject, then, this point emerges clearly: that though the heresy which is mere error should be combatted with spiritual weapons only, the secular rulers have the right, in cases of extreme danger, to suppress heresy that shows itself in sedition leading to riots, revolt and schism, by legal means and by imposing the penalties prescribed in the law of the land. In a well-known passage, later condemned by the University of Paris, he implied this distinction: "Nor did he [Augustine] condemn if God inspired the minds of princes to coerce those who disturbed the tranquility of the Church. But whoever heard of orthodox bishops inciting kings to the slaughter of heretics who were nothing but heretics?"[110]

This is substantially the position of the Utopians: heresy in itself is beyond the interest and reach of the secular power; and heresy in itself will not be punished, but the heretic, when acting in a way that shakes the foundations of society, will be punished, but not as a heretic; the heretic will be punished for the crime of sedition, riot, or whatever the crime that may be proved against him, under laws generally applicable to all situations and without regard to religious beliefs.

IX

Thus we see that the principle that legislation must have a secular purpose if it is to be upheld as constitutional under the First Amendment has its roots in many centuries of history. Perhaps the first conscious movement toward its formulation was in the *Sunday-Closing* case, *McGowan* v. *Maryland*,[111] in which Chief Justice Warren said that the Establishment Clause

does not ban federal or state regulation of conduct whose reason or effect merely happens to coincide or harmonize with the tenets of some or all religions. In many instances, the Congress or state legislatures conclude that the general welfare of society, wholly apart from any religious considerations, demands such regulation. Thus, for temporal purposes, murder is illegal. And the fact that this agrees with the Judaeo-Christian religions while it may disagree with others does not invalidate the regulation. So too with the questions of adultery and polygamy. . . . The same could be said of theft, fraud, etc., because those offenses were also proscribed in the Decalogue.

While the Court in *McGowan* v. *Maryland* was concerned with the Establishment Clause, the above reasoning would apply just as well to legislation challenged under the Free Exercise Clause. In the companion case *Braunfeld* v. *Brown*,[112] which involved a question of religious liberty and was argued by a merchant who observed the seventh day as his Sabbath, Chief Justice Warren said:

If the purpose or effect of a law is to impede the observance of one or all religions or to discriminate invidiously between religions, that law is constitutionally invalid even though the burden may be characterized as being only indirect. But if the State regulates conduct by enacting a general law within its power, the purpose and effect of which is to advance the State's secular goals, the statute is valid despite its indirect burden on religious observance unless the State may accomplish its purpose by means which do not impose such a burden.

Thus constitutional law has adopted a principle of liberty of conscience, which has been transmitted from ancient times —a principle rooted in Biblical and other ancient traditions and history, and transmitted through a long line of martyrs and thinkers, from the Hebrew midwives in Egypt, from Antigone and Socrates, through Castellio, Thomas More, and Erasmus, through John Locke, down to our own day.

But constitutional law has refined and enhanced the principle. First, an act, to meet the test of the First Amendment, must reflect a secular legislative purpose. That, as we have seen, is the bedrock principle. But now more must be shown if the legislation is to be constitutionally sustained. Second, it must be shown that its primary effect is not to inhibit religion. Third, that the administration of the law does not entail an excessive government entanglement with religion. Fourth, that the administration of the act does not inhibit the free exercise of religion.[113] Fifth, it must be shown that the state cannot accomplish its purpose by another means which will not impose a burden on the exercise of religious liberty.[114] Sixth, where the state successfully satisfies the first test (the statute reflects a secular legislative purpose) yet incidentally a burden is imposed on the free exercise of religion, the infringement must be justified by "a compelling state interest,"[115] that is, "only those interests of the highest order and those not otherwise served can overbalance legitimate claims to the free exercise of religion";[116] in effect, the conduct or actions regulated must be shown to have posed "some substantial threat to public safety, peace, or order."[117]

5

Individual Conscience
or Group Consciousness:
Religious Liberty in
the United States and Israel

IT HAS HAPPENED more than once when I discussed with Americans in Israel, or with Israelis who have a Western background, my impressions of things I have seen at the Kotel (the Western Wall), that my friends' first reactions to anything I may have said were to object to the *mehitza* (the fence that separates men and women). The objection to the separation is not stated dispassionately but with strong, deep feeling, as if a personal affront were involved. Then I would gently suggest that the pious men who worship at the Wall generally do so in *minyanim* (congregations made up of at least ten male adults), that they are men who interpret the Halakhah as requiring, under such circumstances, a physical barrier that separates the sexes. "Well, then," the usual rejoinder has been, "the men should never have been allowed to *daven* (pray) in *minyanim* at the Wall. They should pray individually." Usually I do not pursue the discussion beyond this point: but if I were

to push the argument, I would point out that the reminder—
"Let them pray individually but not in a *minyan*!"—reveals a
basic philosophical, religious, and psychological difference between my friends whose spontaneous approach is Western, and
the traditionalist Jew whose presence dominates the scene at
the Wall. These differences are deep and significant, and an
understanding of them will, I hope, shed light on the tangled
and abrasive issues of religious liberty in both Israel and the
United States, but especially in Israel.

I shall devote more time to the traditionalist position because
that position is hardly known, except superficially, by persons
whose minds are dominated by Western ideals and Western
categories of thought. I shall, in my overall treatment of the subject, try to be just to both parties; for I myself, I might as well
admit at the outset, have been nurtured by both cultures and
am compelled to think of myself as a kind of Hellenistic Jew,
one who early in his life came under the strong influence of
Philo and Maimonides, philosophers who tended to seek points
of agreement rather than disagreement between cultures and
philosophies and to look for what they could ingest rather than
expel, accommodate rather than destroy.

I

The overwhelming majority of Jews who worship at the
Wall worship not as *individual Jews* but as components of Jewry. Almost always when I came to the Wall a man approached
me and asked if I would not join a *minyan* that was then being
formed. If I had told him that I preferred to *daven* by myself, he
would, I am sure, have looked upon me with disbelief.

First of all, if it is a Shabbat or a holiday, or a Monday or
Thursday morning, or the beginning of a new month (Rosh
Hodesh), there will be a reading from the Torah scroll, and this
is permitted only for a *minyan*. The Torah reading is the center

of the service, around which the other elements are clustered. No private reading of the Torah can possibly play the same role as the public reading, for the congregational reading is a public affirmation of the revelation to all Israel, and to each Israelite as a member of universal Jewry (Klal Yisroel), which includes the countless generations of the past and future, as well as all who are alive and scattered among the nations of the world. The public reading is a recollection of the past, a prophecy of the future, and a present renewal—as though all Israel were compressed into the *minyan* and cried out with the cry heard at Sinai: "*We* will do and *we* will listen!" (*naaseh venishma*).[1]

Not just the reading of the Torah but also some of the most essential elements of the liturgy are permitted only when worship is with a *minyan*. Thus the *Kedusha*, the *Kaddish*, the *Borkhu*, and the priestly blessing may be recited only when there is a *minyan*.

It should be noted, too, that the contents of the prayers, whether recited privately or in a congregation, are in the plural form. They are prayers offered for *Jewry and not for oneself*.[2] The only noteworthy exceptions in the daily liturgy are two prayers, and these are ethical in content and spirit, and are not petitions for any tangible things.[3] Even on Yom Kippur, the great confessionals that are recited are not focused on the individual Jew's sins but on sins that anyone of the total congregation of Israel may have committed anywhere.

In all these ways we see that for thousands of years the synagogue has taught Jews to see themselves as one single body, of which each Jew is to see himself as a member; that each Jew is to pursue his own life and interests only in such a way that they will further the life and interests of Jewry; that the sin committed by one Jew taints the whole body of Jewry, which must confess that sin and cleanse itself of it; that the joy or distress of one Jew is the joy or distress of Klal Yisroel. As Martin Buber summarized this lesson of the synagogue: When a man prays, and even when he prays alone in his room, he must first unite with Israel, for in every true prayer it is the community—and not the individual—that is praying. A prayer not spoken *beshem Kol Yisroel* (in the name of Israel) is no prayer at all.[4]

On one of my visits in Jerusalem I witnessed a living manifestation of this truth. On the last day of Passover I participated in one of numerous *minyanim* at the Wall, in a *minyan* made up of Hasidim and Mitnaggedim, Sephardim and Ashkenazim. We all stood around the table as the Torah was read by a clean-shaven man dressed in Western style. The portion he read was the Song of Moses from Exodus (*Oz yosheer Moshe*).[5] He read the words with such feeling and such beauty of tone that his face became transfigured, and men in kaftans and fur hats, and men, like myself, dressed in Western style, stood and listened in rapt attention to the words as though we had never before heard them:

The Lord is a man of war;
The Lord is His name.
Pharaoh's chariots and his host
   hath He cast into the sea, . . .
They went down into the depth like a stone. . . .
The enemy said:
"I will pursue, I will overtake, I will
   divide the spoil; . . .
I will draw my sword, my hand shall destroy them". . . .
Thou stretchest out Thy right hand—
The earth swallowed them. . . .
Terror and dread falleth upon them;
By greatness of Thine arm
   they are as still as a stone. . . .

Now, whenever I recite or hear the Song of Moses, I hear the words as they were chanted by this anonymous reader at the Wall on the last day of Passover, and I see again his face and the faces of the men who made a circle around him, faces that seemed to say that the song was chanted on behalf of and in response to all Israel: a timeless chant that celebrates the past, prophesizes the future, and signifies the present. No *private* reading of the song, in one's home, or even at the Wall, could have given it this meaning. Its meaning was a creative event produced by the confluence of individual Jews who spontaneously formed themselves into an *edah*, a congregation of witnesses representative of all Israel—with its history and traditions, its present despairs and victories, and its future promises, destiny, and hopes.

The subtle but ineluctable intertwining of individual Jew with Jewry can be felt in the synagogue even when the congregation chants Psalms that speak in the first person singular, as many Psalms do. In the great Psalm 130, a typical case, the Jew seems to speak of and for himself, yet he speaks also, and chiefly, of and for Israel:

Out of the depth have I called Thee, O Lord.
Lord, harken unto my voice. . . .

And then the *group* cry becomes explicit:

O, Israel hope in the Lord;
For with the Lord there is mercy . . .
And He will redeem Israel. . . .

The traditional Jew is no detached, rugged individual. Nor is his reality, his essence, completely absorbed in some monstrous collectivity which alone can claim rights and significance. He *is* an individual but one whose essence is determined by the fact that he is a brother, a *fellow Jew*. His prayers are, therefore, communal and not private, integrative and not isolative, holistic and not separative. All Jews, therefore, have the same prayers; they pray at the same times; they pray toward the same place; and, as George Foot Moore has said, summarizing normative Judaism, all Jews, when they pray, in spirit are in *one* place,[6] and, I would add, in spirit are in *one* time.

In the *Kuzari* Judah Halevi deals admirably with this whole

question of private versus public prayer. He explains why prayer should be common. First, a community will never pray for
anything that will be harmful to the individual, but the reverse
is not at all true, for individuals would pray for things hurtful to
some others.* Second, an individual rarely accomplishes his
prayers without slips and errors. When, however, he prays with
a *minyan*, each makes up for the forgetfulness or error of the
other. In this way a complete prayer is offered up. "A person,"
Judah Halevi says, "who prays for himself is like one who retires
alone into his house, refusing to assist his fellow citizens in the
repair of their walls. . . . He, however, who joins the majority
spends little yet remains in safety, because one replaces the de-
fects of the others." By praying by and for himself, a man sins
against the community, but even more, says Judah Halevi, he
sins against *himself*. "For the relation of the individual is as the
relation of the single limb to the body. In case bleeding is required, should the arm refuse to give its blood, then the whole
body, including the arm, would suffer."[7]

In this passage Judah Halevi affirms that which is the teaching of traditional Judaism: that no Jew is an island unto himself;
that always he is a *fellow Jew*; that just as nine *fellow Jews* need
him to make a *minyan*, even so he needs them; that outside of
Jewry, there are no Jews; that though, as a man, a Jew is an
individual who has individual rights, as a Jew his nature is not
private but communal; *that it is not the Jew but Jewry that
brings the service of prayer*.

Almost every Jewish thinker, writing in the classical tradition, saw and felt the same overwhelming preeminence of Jewry over the Jew. Thus, to take one other example, because of its
focus on prayer: Albo pointed out that the prayer of Moses that
he be permitted to enter the Promised Land was not granted,

---

*Halevi might have illustrated this point by citing the fact that on Yom Kippur
the High Priest when he left the Holy of Holies closed his prayers with the
words: "Pay no heed to the prayers of travellers (who pray that there be no rain)"
(Midrash Rabbah, Leviticus, Soncino, 256).

but when he prayed for Israel after the Israelites had worshiped the golden calf, his prayer was accepted. There is, then, said Albo, a difference between the prayer of an individual for himself and his prayer for the congregation. Although the two prayers may be of the same kind, yet, said Albo, the prayer for the congregation is more likely to be heard. Therefore, "the rabbis say: 'God does not reject the prayers of the congregation. . . .' They also say: 'A person should always join a congregation,' thus indicating that the prayer of a congregation—the *tephilah haklal* —is always accepted while that of an individual is not."[8]

I would offer as a lovely symbol of this preeminently significant characteristic of traditional Judaism what the ancient rabbis did when it came to approving a prayer to be recited by travelers. At times a man had to go on a journey, and often he traveled alone on hazardous roads and highways, and a pious Jew would tend naturally to pray for his safety and safe return. But the rabbis taught that even under such circumstances a man must associate others with himself in his petitions—even a solitary wayfarer must pray, not "Lead *me* in safety," but "Lead *us* in safety."[9]

Thus, in these and other ways, the world of prayer in which the Jew was enmeshed trained and molded him to think and feel, in all his moments and actions, as an intimate part of the organic entity known as Klal Yisroel.

II

In my discussion of the traditional Jew, I have avoided using the term "Orthodox Jew," because, when judged against what I have said about group consciousness in traditional Judaism, today many Orthodox Jews are not traditional, and some non-Orthodox Jews are, in fact, traditional.

For the categories of thought and feeling of the nontraditional Jew—whether Orthodox, Conservative, Reform, Humanist, or whatever—are derivatively Western, flowing mainly out of the Renaissance, the Reformation, and the Enlightenment. To such a Jew, Judaism is a religion but not the whole of life; and religion to him is strictly and absolutely a personal, private affair. He considers himself, basically, a Jew by choice or preference, for he is free to discard religion altogether or to change his religion for another. He is a nominalist as to Jewry, for the only real entities he knows are individual Jews. Together with other Jews, he may join or organize a congregation as a purely voluntary association, just as he may or may not join the Chamber of Commerce or a fraternal order. The congregation to him is not a *Gemeinschaft*, a natural group like the family, but a *Gesellschaft*, a contrived, made-to-order association.[10] His emphasis is on religious *liberty* and not on religious *duty*. He believes that *private* prayer or worship may be more significant than congregational (*tefilah be-zibur*). He walks into his *Bet Knesset*, his synagogue or temple, as he would into a movie theatre—he has paid for his seat, and he expects the cantor and the rabbi to "conduct the service," in which he "participates," mainly, however, as a passive listener; and the psychic distance between him and the person in the seat next to him may be, indeed, very great.

Of course the Western Jew knows that he is not the only Jew, and, as we know from recent experience, in moments of grave crisis he feels a sense of identity with other Jews whose existence may be threatened; but I do not believe that such moments and the responses they evoke change the purely associative character of his identification with other Jews. He remains a Jew, in his own mind, by voluntary choice and not by will or grace of God; and Judaism remains for him a purely private affair, from which he can extricate himself at will. It is baggage which he needs or which he can declare to be unnecessary; and in the free society in which he lives, he can either carry it or leave it, without let or hindrance.

Since religion is to a Jew a purely personal matter, like his love for his wife or his love of poetry, art, or music, he believes that his prayer should be not only a personal experience but also a personal communication from himself; thus he naturally finds little if any "relevance" in the traditional liturgy; he would like to see new prayers, new forms of worship constantly developed; he demands new wine in new bottles.

Jewish organic, group consciousness was nurtured in the Diaspora by exposure of Jews to common enemies, common fears, and threats; by the forced living in close quarters within ghetto walls. These were external forces. There were, however, inner spiritual forces that contributed greatly to the formation of each person's consciousness—the need to live together in order to have a *shohet*, a *mohel*, a *mikvah*,[11] a teacher, a sacred burial place, and a *hevrah kadishah*[12] and, as we have seen, the Jew needed at least nine other adult male Jews to constitute a Jewish community for prayer and worship. These basic needs ruled out the possibility of the development of religion as a purely private matter.

A significant effect of both these outer and inner forces was the almost total urbanization of the Jew. But this development, intimately related, as both cause and effect, to Jewish group consciousness, in due course exposed the Jew to the full impact of the individualizing strains in the Renaissance, the Protestant Reformation, and the Enlightenment, and even more to the sweep of the Industrial Revolution and capitalism. One can safety make these judgments, I believe, without necessarily subscribing to theories regarding the affinity between Judaism and capitalism. In any case, as the urban Jews have achieved relative freedom from fear and have won relative economic security and affluence, they have lost much of their group consciousness and have become individualists and individualistic Jews.

III

We have presented two different and contradictory types—the traditionalist or corporate Jew, who dominated Jewish life and values for many centuries and who alone held the stage of Jewish history until the nineteenth century; and the individualist Jew, who during the last century and a half, has moved into a position of dominance. Jews do not always, however, represent one extreme type or the other; some can be characterized as having two minds, or as striving, consciously or unconsciously, to assimilate one type to the other.

In the State of Israel there are nonreligious *kibbutzim* where the members have transferred into the secular realm the group consciousness of the traditionalist Jew, and have even extended it to encompass the economic realm and a substantial part of family life—outreachings of the group consciousness that were beyond the historic forms that we had known. It was in part for this reason, I believe, that Chief Rabbi Kook felt a closer affinity with some secularist *kibbutzniks* than he did with some Orthodox Jews.

In the United States and in Israel I know secularist, even antireligious Jews, who think, feel, celebrate, and suffer as members of Jewry, while in other respects they manifest the essential marks of the individualist; and I know observant Jews in the United States who hardly ever think or act as Jews who are participants in the group consciousness of Jewry. The picture is an extremely complex one, but still, as I have tried to show, some generalizations are possible.

I wish now to test the contrast between the two types against the sense of individual and group responsibility.

At the Wall one Sabbath morning in the middle of the service, someone who was in the *minyan*—a man of about forty, bearded, dressed in a black kaftan, covered over by a large *tallit* (prayer shawl)—cried out and waved a hand threateningly in the direction of the passageway to the Temple Mount, above the section reserved for women. Although there was posted in the area a warning against taking photographs on the Sabbath or holidays, apparently this worshiper saw some tourists above who were getting their cameras ready. When I looked up in the direction he faced and pointed to, I saw some men and women on top looking bewildered, for they had seen the man's gesture. Then the man walked over to someone in the *minyan* who obviously came out of a different environment—he had a short, trimmed beard, wore a Western-style suit and a tie, and a medium-size *tallit*. I happened to be standing near to both men as they came together. The man who had cried out explained in Yiddish that he had seen someone who wanted to take a photograph. The other looked at him and said: *"Chaim, vos hart es dir?"* ("What business is it of yours?"). Chaim shrugged his shoulders, flushed in inexpressible anger, and hurried away.

In this little drama I saw played out the conflict between the two types we have been discussing. The man who cried out had acted on the principle that most effectively expresses the group consciousness of Jewry—the principle as stated in the Talmud, that all Israelites are sureties for one another, that each is responsible for all others (*Kol Yisroel arevim ze-elze*).[13] As stated in one place in the Talmud:

> Whoever is able to protest against the wrongdoings of his family and fails to do so is punished for the family's wrongdoings. Whoever is able to protest against the wrongdoings of his fellow citizens and does not do so is punished for the wrongdoings of the people of his city. Whoever is able to protest against the wrongdoings of the world and does not do so is punished for the wrongdoings of the world.[14]

The *Mekilta de-Rabbi Ishmael* asks why is Israel compared to a lamb? "What is the nature of a lamb? If it is hurt in one limb, all its limbs feel the pain. So also are the people of Israel. One of them commits a sin and all of them suffer from the punishment."[15] Obviously, if all are affected by what anyone does, all must be concerned by what each one does. For we are "members of one another."

Maimonides universalized this sense of vicarious, corporate responsibility, this commandment to care about what each and every other Jew does. It is necessary, he said,

> that every one, throughout the year, should regard himself as if he were half innocent and half guilty, and should regard the whole of mankind (and not merely Israel) as half innocent and half guilty. If then he commits one more sin, he presses down the scale of guilt against himself and the whole world (not Israel alone) and causes his destruction. If he fulfills one commandment, he turns the scale of merit in his favor, and the favor of the whole world, and brings salvation and deliverance to all his fellow-creatures and to himself, as it is said, "the righteous man is the foundation of the world"; that is to say, he who acts justly presses down the scale of merit in favor of all the world and saves it.[16]

I know of no statement in religious literature that more effectively identifies the individual and his actions with the destiny of all mankind; and yet this statement only fulfills what is implied in Jewish group consciousness, in the sense of moral interdependence and mutual moral responsibility, in the conception that every Israelite is responsible to and for all Israel. This consciousness does not reduce but rather enhances and accentuates the dignity and power of the individual. Although an integral part of an organic whole, from which he cannot be separated, except at the cost of his moral and spiritual life, let each man say, with Hillel, "If I am here, then everyone is here."[17]

Now, to return to the scene at the Wall, the traditionalist Jew instinctively acted on the principle of reciprocal responsibility, for he saw someone who was about to desecrate the Sabbath, and he felt that it was *his duty* to try to prevent the act. His Western friend, however, felt no such responsibility or call of duty. He carried over from the legal to the moral and religious realms the principle of exclusively individual responsibility, as formulated by Ezekiel: "The soul that sinneth, it shall die . . .

the righteousness of the righteous shall be upon himself and the wickedness of the wicked shall be upon himself."[18]

In the United States, where the individualist principle is supreme, the Jews, except in a grave crisis, tend to follow the line of thought on which the question, "*Vos hart es dir?*" was based. Each Jew is encased in his privacy, and what he does, while it may be the concern of the government, is supposed to be no one else's business. The American Jew, like his Gentile neighbour, believes that the safest principle is, "Live and let live!"

In Israel, however, the matter is more complicated. The young people in Mea'h Shearim or B'nai Berak who overturn or throw stones at cars moving on the Sabbath act on the principle that all Israelites are responsible for one another. They act out their group consciousness, the feeling of group solidarity that is deeply rooted in their minds and souls. By acting to stop a Jew from sinning, they believe that they are acting *to stop themselves from sinning, for their inaction in the face of wrongdoing would itself be a wrongdoing*. The underlying idea is that all Jews, children of the same patriarchs, are brothers, and a brother ought not to say, "*Vos hart es dir?*" For it *is* his business to interfere when he sees his brother engaged in a transgression. If a man eats sour grapes, will not his brother's teeth be set on edge? The wickedness of the wicked is upon him who is wicked, *but it is also upon his brother*. The traditionalists may be alienated from the world; but they have their own world, the Jewish world, in which they are not alienated from one another.

IV

The contest in Israel over control of personal status may be interpreted as one between the two types of consciousness as we have described them.

The clash between these two approaches can be seen clearly

in the debate generated by the *Benjamin Shalit* case.[19] When David Ben-Gurion discussed the case before the Central Conference of American Rabbis at the Hebrew University on March 8, 1970, he said that if the matter were left to him, the law in Israel would be simply that a Jew is anyone who says that he wants to be considered a Jew. No questions should be asked except such as would tend to make sure that the claim is not made for some criminal or fraudulent purpose.

Now, I find this to be a prime example of the individualistic, Western approach. Starting from the premise that religion is strictly a private affair, it follows that religion and religious affiliation should be left exclusively to one's own conscience. This, years ago, was the position maintained by Chaim Zhitlowsky, who carried it so far as to maintain that if a Jew becomes convinced of the truth of Christianity, there is no reason why he could not be accepted as a Christian Jew, just as we accept an atheist Jew. Ben-Gurion, I suspect, would have drawn the line against the apostate, just as the Israel Supreme Court did in the case of Brother Daniel.[20]

The traditionalist, on the other hand, relies on the Jewish mother to provide an undeniable link between the individual and Jewry. This view by-passes, as a matter of relative unimportance, the subjective wishes of the person. Having in mind the famous formula of Sir Henry Maine, we might say that while the individualist would maximize the movement from status to contract, the traditionalist would insist on maximizing the movement from contract to status.

As to conversion, the individualistic approach is to make the process as easy and expeditious as possible. If a Jew wishes to marry a non-Jew, the wishes of the couple should be, according to the individualistic approach, controlling. Thus, Ben-Gurion related that when his son decided to marry a non-Jewish girl, Ben-Gurion sought out a liberal rabbi who would declare her a Jew without subjecting her to the requirements of the Halakhah. Essentially, from this point of view, conversion is a unilateral action, fundamentally of a subjective character; one simply elects himself into Jewry.

It is far different for the traditionalist. To him conversion is a good deal like the process of child adoption. The man and woman who wish to adopt a child move cautiously, prudently, and the adoption agency and the court give careful consideration to objective as well as subjective factors. The Halakhah essentially has the same attitude toward conversion, for it poses before itself someone who, if adopted, would be a member of the family of Abraham, Isaac, and Jacob—*their* child, just as if he had been born to parents who, undeniably, are Jews. The traditionalist surely knows that, after conversion, the new Jew may follow his own erratic ways, just as do many who are sons or daughters of Jewish parents; but just as parents are not exempt from the duty of teaching their children, so, too, are the rabbis not exempt from teaching the non-Jew who wishes to become a son or daughter of Abraham, Isaac, and Jacob.

Thus, in brief, what is controlling to the individualist is the fact that the non-Jew is willing to become a Jewish spouse; he sees but a few persons who are affected by the decision; for the rest, he feels that it is none of their business, for religion is a private matter, and it has been satisfactorily settled privately. The traditionalist, however, sees not only the persons immediately affected, but Jewry as a whole. He feels that he carries the full weight of the Jewish tradition; he feels that he holds in his hands the integrity of Klal Yisroel; that he is the bearer of the inheritance, which he is asked to transmit to a non-Jew who is an applicant for admission into the Jewish family. And he sees not only the applicant, but his sons and daughters, and their children, and their children's children to the end of days. It is an awesome matter, indeed, for the traditionalist, who thinks of himself as representative of the body and spirit, the past and future, of Israel. To him, Jewry is a God-ordained community, and not a free association of self-elected members; a *Gemeinschaft*, and not a *Gesellschaft*; a home and not a motel.[21]

V

What we have discussed and exemplified is the fact that within Judaism there are different gates of understanding and different paths of wisdom. In the United States, Jews are divided into Orthodox, Conservative, and Reform, and into religious and secularist groupings; but except for certain Hasidic enclaves and some scattered individuals, American Jews, like Americans generally, are thoroughly individualistic. Jews cooperate for common causes, but Jewish organizations, including even Orthodox congregations, are like the United Nations Organization—each member is a sovereign entity, who associates with other members as kings and queens may associate with one another. There are church-state problems, but they are problems between Jewish groups, on the one hand, and the federal and state governments, on the other; with some recent exceptions, church-state problems have tended to unite rather than to divide American Jews.[22]

In Israel, however, Jews seem to be more decisively divided into individualists and traditionalists. This division, as we have seen, has deep psychic roots. The conflicts between these camps have at times been translated, by individualists, into church-state problems; but to the traditionalist this translation makes no sense, for to him Judaism is all-embracing, his Judaism does not allow him to divide Israeli concerns into fixed sacred and secular departments. I believe that clarification is not advanced at this time by the translation of the Israeli conflicts into the Western categories of church and state. For we are dealing here, as we have seen, not with theories or abstract principles, but with ways of life, with life styles, with deeply rooted ways of thought and feeling.

The differences between Israeli individualists and traditionalists often cut across the differences between the religious and the nonreligious, for there are nonreligious, even anticlerical,

Israelis who tend to approve, though with mixed feelings, the relative quiet of the Sabbath, and a rather restrictive, though somewhat modified, halakhic definition of who is a Jew. The traditionalist Israeli, religious or nonreligious, finds it difficult, if not impossible, to divide Israel definitively between God and Caesar, when Caesar himself belongs to God's people.

The primary need in Israel, if I may be permitted to submit my own opinion, is for mutual understanding—a by no means easy thing to achieve. One of the greatest intellectual and spiritual achievements of the ancient rabbis came when they were able to say, meaningfully, as to the differences between two schools of thought: "Both these and the others are words of the living God" (*"Elu ve-elu divrei Elokim hayyim"*).[23]

In Israel, both sides are right in what they affirm, and wrong in what they deny. In due time, if they can in the meantime exercise a high degree of toleration and self-control, they may reach a point of confluence, and create a way still unknown to us. The two sides may discover that there are supreme values in both the individualist and the traditionalist-corporate approaches to Jewish identity and life, and a new form of Jewish reality may yet emerge—one from which will be removed all that is merely exigent and adventitious, and which will conserve all that enlarges and enhances life and its promises.

In the meantime one feels like asking: If Jews can learn to live with non-Jews, why can't they learn to live with Jews? Yet often one hears remarks that show deeply ingrained distrust and even contempt for other Jews. For example, one often hears an Israeli with a Western orientation make unpleasant remarks about the style of dress of an Israeli Hassid—his earlocks, his stockings, his black felt hat, or *streimel* (fur hat). I wonder if these critics would feel the same way toward the Amish or Mennonite farmers in Pennsylvania or Ontario, or if they have the same feeling of revulsion for the dress of Greek or Russian Orthodox priests who are seen on streets in Jerusalem. Whatever the origin of the Hassid's hair style and dress, his motivation is to guard himself against following the customs of the non-Jews, and he thus observes, admittedly in an extreme way, the principle of *chukot ha-goy*.[24] But is not Zionism itself founded on this principle of marking the Jew off from the non-Jew, a principle which may be differently interpreted and applied by men of different ideals, temperaments, and backgrounds?

We have a blindness, William James observed, in regard to the feelings of people different from ourselves, which accounts for, he said, "the stupidity and injustice of our opinions, so far as they deal with the significance of alien lives."[25]

The feeling of strangeness is, of course, mutual, and the distrust and contempt are almost always, I suspect, reciprocated. Neither side sees the inner life of the other but only the outer garments, the appearances—one sees only the long kaftan, the other sees only the miniskirt, and these are taken as if they were representative of the whole person.

Solomon Schechter pointed out that the Jew was the world's first nonconformist and that Judaism is a protesting religion.[26] It remains to be seen how far the Jews, who are nonconformist in the eyes of their neighbors, can live their Jewish life fully and freely among fellow Jews from whom they differ in both beliefs and practice, both outer appearance and inner reality. We ask from the non-Jew the right *for ourselves* to be different. This right to be different, I submit, like charity, should begin at home. And Israel *is* home; for Robert Frost was quite right: Home is the place where they must take you in when you have no place else to go. Is not this the essential idea enshrined in Israel's Law of Return?[27]

The easiest thing to do is to think in terms of the implacable opposition between two sets of ideals. One may recall here the bitter enmity of the Mitnaggedim and the Hasidim in the eighteenth and nineteenth centuries. Many who are impressed by the polarity of the two positions we have discussed see a *Kultur-*

kampf as inevitable, and some think that the sooner it comes, the better.

But there is nothing that can be more devastating to a people than a religious war. Consider Belfast today and see how Catholic and Protestant lay waste to people's lives and to a country.

The issues between the individualist and the traditionalist in Israel will not be settled by warfare on the streets, or by rock-throwing, or by violent demonstrations. Each side stands for ideals that are too valuable to be destroyed by passion, resentment, and anger. It is no abandonment or disloyalty to one's ideals to limit oneself to discussion and peaceful negotiation for their acceptance or accommodation. But a commitment not to resort to passion and violence implies a readiness to offer and accept compromises—compromises which yet preserve the integrity of the ideal as a hope and a goal.

An example of such a compromise—one which preserves the best of competing values and which yet leaves alone the integrity of ideals for possible later vindication—may be the decision of the Israel Supreme Court in the case of Brother Daniel. From the standpoint of the ideal of religious liberty, a Jew should be able to have whatever religious beliefs he wishes —he could believe in the existence and power of Satan, angels, and demons, or whatever. Brother Daniel, adopting the argument of Thomas Jefferson, could have contended that his belief in Jesus as the Messiah does not pick another Jew's pocket nor break another Jew's leg;[28] it was, therefore, beyond the reach of any official inquest under the Law of Return or any other law in a society that claims to be free. Indeed, from the standpoint of traditionalism, if it were to be guided by Halakhah, Brother Daniel, born of a Jewish mother, was a Jew regardless of his Christian beliefs. We can see here, how, contrary to appearances, the traditionalist position in fact stood for maximum freedom of belief, since beliefs are irrelevant to the question of who is a Jew. The majority of the court, however, side-stepped both the Halakhah and the individualistic principle and found the answer in a Jewish group-consciousness that transcended both the Halakhah and the individualistic ideology. Regardless of theory and definitions, the Jewish consciousness as found by the court seems to say that it is impossible to separate completely Jewish ethnicity and Jewish religion. If this is so, then the conclusion follows that at least in one important repect an individualist Jew cannot claim as absolutes religious liberty or the principle of separation of church and state. At some point an objective test intervenes and displaces subjectivity; at some point status makes contract irrelevant.

In appearance the extremes are far apart. The traditionalist, paradoxically, spiritualizes secular phenomena: for example, the mother's religion determines the religion of the child; ethnicity, or peoplehood, is an inseparable aspect of Jewry. The individualist, paradoxically, secularizes spiritual phenomena: for example, subjectivity, belief, or loyalty to an idea or a value is a ticket of admission into peoplehood. Yet what overrides all differences and provides an underlying unity is the will to live as a Jew and as part of a single people. This is the teleological fact which ignores all distinctions and gives the character of ultimate illusion to the conflict. Neither side should permit any step toward a breach in that unity, such as Jewry suffered when it split into the peoples of Judea and Israel, or into Jews and Karaites. The flux of the two groups, now virtually two societies, into a single community which would preserve all that is valuable in each, is the greatest test of Israel's creative spirit.

The days of the *herem* (ban of excommunication) are over. This is the lesson the religious traditionalists should learn from the ban on Hasidism imposed in 1772 by the Gaon of Vilna. For some years Mitnaggedim would not marry Hasidim, but before long the forces of life and experience proved stronger than the *herem* of the Gaon. Today there is no such Gaon, and the ghetto and the sanctions it found effective have disappeared. Resort to Knesset legislation as a substitute for the *herem* can be useful as a temporary and temporizing measure, but sooner or later all parties concerned must learn that there are limits on what can be coerced and that there are, in fact, some things that one must simply learn to live with, things which are beyond the reach of law or of other men's wills.

With respect to all such matters, the advice of William James is, I believe, the best that wisdom has to offer: "Hands off: neither the whole of truth nor the whole of good is revealed to any single observer, although each observer gains a partial superiority of insight from the peculiar position in which he stands. . . . It is enough to ask of each of us that he be faithful to his own opportunities and make the most of his own blessings, without presuming to regulate the rest of the vast field."[29]

Both sides can lay claim to the ideal of liberty. But they mean different things by liberty. One side means freedom from external, especially governmental, coercion. The other side means freedom to labor in the Torah.[30] But neither side can have its way fully without force, suppression, and oppression. We can say to both: *Lo zeh a-derech!* (This is not the way!). For if people should try to fulfill their ideals, come hell or high water, hell and high water will soon overtake their world. For with people's ideals it is the same as with their diets: what is one man's food is another man's poison. People do not, and will not, agree on their ideals. This is why Plato wisely left it to people to see their ideals in all their perfection only in heaven. Here on this earth there is the possibility only for approximations, intimations, and accommodations.

6

From Jewish Rights
to Human Rights

WHAT I SHALL DISCUSS falls naturally into three parts: first, I shall examine the little-known facts concerning Jewish self-defense efforts in czarist Russia following the pogroms of 1881–1882 and the Homel and Kishinev pogroms of 1903, in which the threatened populations defended their lives and property with primitive weapons and guns; second, I shall discuss the Jewish organizations that were created in the last century to defend Jewish rights by resort to political action and propaganda—organizations formed chiefly in Western Europe and the United States on behalf of threatened Jewish communities in Russia and other countries where Jews were exposed to persecution; and third, how the Jewish defense organizations in the United States moved from the defense of Jewish rights to the defense of fundamental human rights, from the rights of Jews to the rights of Everyman. Their concern remains Jewish rights, but these are seen as encompassing the fundamental rights of all human beings, just as the Halakhah extended the moral duty of *hesed* (kindness) from Jew to stranger to all humanity. In this movement of extension one can find an articulation in life of the great principle formulated by Hillel in the *Pirke Aboth* (I, 14): "If I am not for myself, then who will be for me? But if I am for myself alone, then what am I? And if not now, when?"

I

      In the last century—a period of great contrasts of darkness and light for the Jewish people—the Jews have resorted to just about every means available to a weak minority threatened with death or with deprivation of basic human rights.

      In the Russian pogroms, the victims seldom exercised the fundamental human right of self-defense, for a number of very good reasons. First of all, the Jews had learned from bitter experience that often attempts at self-defense only aggravated their plight; for the mob at first might have been satisfied with plunder and beatings, but the sight of Jews wielding arms, or even only tools or pots and pans, and threatening to use them against the mob, tended to incite to greater brutality and even murder. Second, when Jews acted in self-defense, they were then charged with having intended to commit atrocities against the non-Jews of the city or town, so that the Jews became the aggressors, and the "pogromchiks" became the innocent victims. For example, soon after the pogrom in Kishinev in 1903, the Jews of Homel—a city of which half of the population of forty thousand was Jewish—decided that if they were to be attacked, they would defend themselves. A pogrom did take place, in which the mob was aided by government troops. When the pogrom was over, more self-defending Jews than attacking mobsters were arrested, and the government report made it appear that the events were brought about by an attack of Jews on Christian residents and upon the government troops, in consequence of which the Christians and the troops were forced to act in self-defense. The cause of the disorders, the report concluded, "lies in the extremely hostile and defiant attitude of the local Jews toward the Christians." Third, the appearance of

Jews in a stance that showed a readiness to defend themselves provided an excuse for calling in troops to put down a Jewish insurrection; and thus the government aided the rioters, not merely passively, by standing by and failing to protect the lives and property of Jews, but actively and aggressively by joining in the murder, robbery, and other crimes. To use the Homel pogrom again as an example, in 1904, a year after the pogrom, the government handed down an indictment according to which the Jews of Homel, wishing to avenge the Kishinev massacre, had taken up arms and attacked the Christian community; the aggressive attitude of the Jews forced the soldiers to shoot at them. Sixty persons were indicted, including thirty-six Jews.

With such experiences in mind, where everything was stacked against the Jewish victims, how could Jewish leaders be expected to promote self-defense as a realistic means of protection of their right to life and security? Yet the remarkable thing is that, though such instances were few in number, self-defense was resorted to and was urged upon the Jewish people of Russia. Thus, in 1881, following the accession of Czar Alexander III, a horde of mobsters arrived at the railway station of Berdychev, where they were met by a group of Jewish guards who, armed with clubs, did not allow the visiting mob to leave the railway cars. "This rare instance of self-defence," wrote Dubnow, "was only made possible by the indulgence of the local police commissioner, or *Ispravnik*, who, for a large consideration, blinked at the endeavor of the Jews to defend themselves against the rioters." In other places, Dubnow added, similar attempts at self-defense were frustrated by the police, and occasionally such attempts at self-defense "made things worse." He cites the events in the town of Konotop, "where, as a result of the self-defence of the Jews, the mob passed from plunder to murder."[1]

The Revolution of 1905 emboldened some Jews to defend themselves when attacked or threatened, but the futility of self-defense against Russian pogroms was made dramatically clear by the tragic events in Zhitomir. When the Jews of that city heard the rumors that they were to be attacked, they began to arm themselves in self-defense, and made their preparations openly. When the attack came, in April 1905, it lasted three days, during which time the Jews were murdered and mutilated. "The Jewish self-defence," wrote Dubnow, "performed prodigies of valor wherever they were not interfered with by the police and military, and died gallantly where the authorities actively assisted the savage work of the infuriated rioters." The murderers were actively assisted by the police and the soldiers.[2]

During the pogroms of 1881–1882 Jewish self-defense was resorted to spontaneously, but the Homel and Kishinev pogroms in 1903 stimulated some Zionist and Jewish socialist leaders to think of organized self-defense as a spiritual no less than a physical necessity. Two weeks after the Kishinev pogrom, the Agudat Soferim Ivrim (Hebrew Writers League) issued a statement, prepared by Ahad Ha-Am, that "it is degrading for five million people . . . to stretch out their necks to be slaughtered and to call for help without attempting to protect their property, dignity, and lives with their own hands." The statement called for the establishment of a permanent organization to defend Jews against all attackers throughout Russia wherever Jews may be living, and urged a meeting of communal representatives to effectuate this purpose. Besides Ahad Ha-Am, the statement was signed by Bialik, Dubnow, and several other writers. The Bund (Jewish socialist party) also issued a statement in 1903 which declared that "violence must be answered with violence, wherever it comes from." A collective defense was organized in Odessa, which armed itself with guns, and which, in proclamations, urged the Jewish youth to arm itself. In Yekaterinoslav, the defense was organized by the Po'alei Zion, which raised money and acquired guns and went out to desert islands to practice marksmanship. In Kiev some two hundred students formed themselves into defense units and prepared themselves with sticks, knives, and pistols. Homel set up a self-defense organization, which also developed from the Po'alei Zion group; the citizens were organized along occupational lines; and the Bund had its own unit in that city. There were self-defense organizations also in Minsk, Warsaw, Vilna, and other cities; in 1905, forty-two cities had such defense groups. But their effectiveness was considerably weakened by class and party divisions. In Zhitomir, for instance, there were three separate defense groups, organized by the Bund, the Po'alei Zion, and the "non-labor Zionists." After 1905, as the revolutionary movements waned, the strength of the Jewish self-defense movement lessened.[3]

A small, weak, despised minority, subject to the arbitrary power of an autocratic government and excluded from any of the benefits that are entailed in citizenship in a commonwealth —what recourse have such people when threatened with plunder and murder except to exercise their natural right of self-defense? The least that a man has a right to expect from his government is protection of his life and property; but when the state itself becomes the robber and murderer, then for the victim the social contract has been dissolved, and he can do nothing but act as men do when they are in a condition of war. And this was, of course, the condition that the Jews of Russia faced. But the odds against them were so disproportionately great that their measures of self-defense, heroic as they were, could only prove to be feeble acts of desperation. For them Russia continued to be a state of nature in which they could find "no arts; no letters; no society," and in which they could expect only "continual fear and danger of violent death."[4]

Philosophically and practically, self-defense cannot be limited to the extreme case where the government itself joins the criminal forces in society to threaten men's lives and property. In our own time, and in the United States, we have many examples of the inadequacy of police protection—a condition which compels citizens to organize themselves into self-defense units.

But in these circumstances we see a majority seeking to protect itself against a minority, to prevent single criminals or gangs of criminals from taking over the streets or terrorizing the neighborhood. And in these cases the citizens act with the approval of the police, with the encouragement of the government, and often with financial support from the state. In Pontiac, Michigan, for example, about 150 citizens are organized into a citywide citizens' watch; the members patrol their own neighborhoods, and are armed only with flashlights and citizen-band radios. In Detroit, there are thirty-five organized citizen patrols, and the city has appropriated $30,000 to pay for their expenses. New York City has a budget of $2.5 million to pay the expenses of its anticrime volunteers.[5]

It was as such a band of citizen volunteers that orthodox young Jews of Brooklyn organized in 1968 as the Jewish Defense League. Their purpose was to protect the Jews of their neighborhood from physical attacks by criminal street gangs. But before long the group became a political movement; it adopted the philosophy that the best defense is offense, and it began to use the revolutionary tactics of confrontation, physical abuse, and violence. Obviously the only thing in common between the Jewish Defense League and the self-defense groups organized by the Jews following the pogroms of 1881 and 1903 in czarist Russia is that the Jewish Defense League also claims to be acting in self-defense of Jewish rights; but only an insignificantly small number of Jews are misled by this semantic corruption.

II

In the course of the Revolution of 1905, with the pogroms of 1903 still fresh as bleeding wounds, the leading Jewish communities of Russia—including Kovno (Kaunas), Homel, Vilna, Berdychev, St. Petersburg, Moscow, Odessa—addressed petitions and memorials to the government, demanding a total end to all restrictions and disabilities. They stated that they would not be satisfied with partial measures, with gradualism, but only with full freedom and equality. But the Jewish leaders felt that the momentum for liberation required an effective organization, one that would rise above partisanship and factionalism. In March 1905 at an illegal conference in Vilna such an organization came into being, called the League for the Attainment of Equal Rights for the Jewish People in Russia. Its objective was stated to be "the realization to their full extent of the civil, political, and national rights of the Jewish people in Russia." The League demanded the total civil and political emancipation of the Jews, coupled with "the freedom of national-cultural self-determination in all its manifestations," which was to include communal self-government, freedom of language, and Jewish school education. The central office of the League was located in St. Petersburg; the directing bureau was composed of twenty-two elected members, among whom were Dubnow and Shemaryahu Levin.

According to Dubnow, the League was the first attempt in modern history "to inscribe upon its banner not only the demand for the civil and political, but also for the national emancipation of the Jewish people, the first attempt to obtain liberty for Jewry as a nationality, and not as a mere denominational group, forming part of the dominant nation, as had been the case in Western Europe during the nineteenth century."[6]

But the nationalistic plank was adopted only over the opposition of the antinationalists. The conference was intentionally composed of people with different, and even contradictory, ideologies, so that it might speak for all Russian Jewry; but the heterogeneity was the League's undoing. Levin had attended the Sixth Zionist Congress in 1903 and voted against the Uganda proposal; Dubnow in 1906 formed the Folkspartei as an expression of his Diaspora nationalism; the Bundists, who had organized themselves in 1897, were protagonists of autonomism and placed special emphasis on Yiddish as the national language; then there were the Jewish Socialist Workers' Party, the Jewish Social Democratic Party, Po'alei Zion, and the Zionist Socialist Workers' Party. The factionalism was proof of how deeply ideology was maintained and how seriously it was espoused. "The divergence of views and tactics among the various groups composing the League," Dubnow recorded, "proved stronger than their common interest in the nearest aim." And so, two years after its founding, the League disintegrated and broke into at least four groups.[7]

Although organizationally the League proved to be a failure, its four conventions manifested the fact that overriding all the deep ideological differences was a dominant commitment to political and civil emancipation and equality, communal self-determination, and cultural-national consciousness. Even the Zionists who projected a national home in Palestine agreed that there must be minority rights, national rights, for Jews in the Diaspora. Perhaps the culminating expression of this commitment to national self-determination was the so-called Copenhagen Manifesto, issued in 1918 by the Zionist headquarters, which, though demanding a national home in Palestine, demanded in all other countries full equality of rights and "national autonomy, cultural, social and political, for the Jewish population of countries largely settled by Jews, as well as of all other countries whose Jewish population demands it."[8]

Far different was the approach of the emancipated Jews who, in 1860, had organized the Alliance Israélite Universelle, as an organization to represent the Jews of Western Europe who were interested in the welfare of their co-religionists in Russia, the Ottoman Empire, and elsewhere. They were not Zionists, and they were not interested in winning for themselves or for other Jews the right of national autonomy. What they had in common among themselves and with Jews everywhere was the Jewish religion, and a common history of persecution and suffering. While their own suffering may have ended, at least so they thought, their memory of the suffering continued as a living experience. And what they had in common, further, was a sense of duty toward their persecuted and afflicted brethren, which helped them to win what President Franklin D. Roosevelt in 1941 made famous as the Four Freedoms: freedom from fear, freedom from want, freedom of worship, and freedom of speech and expression (or as much civil liberty as is enjoyed by non-Jewish citizens).

The immediate stimulation for the formation of the Alliance was the *Mortara* case of 1858.[9] The aims of the organization were succinctly stated as "(1) to work everywhere for the emancipation and moral progress of the Jews; (2) to offer effective assistance to Jews suffering from anti-Semitism; and (3) to encourage all publications calculated to promote this aim." The Alliance pioneered in the use and refinement of Jewish diplomatic methods as it intervened on behalf of persecuted Jews. It assisted Jews to emigrate from Russia and Rumania. In the 1860's it fought for equal rights for Swiss Jews, and enlisted the help of the governments of France, Italy, Belgium, and Holland. In 1872 it convened an international conference to consider the plight of Jews in Rumania, with delegates from France, Germany, England, and the United States participating, a meeting presided over by Isaac Crémieux. The Alliance presented the case against Rumania at the Congress of Berlin in 1878, as a result of which the Treaty of Berlin included articles that provided that in Rumania (and in Serbia and Bulgaria as well) "differences of religious belief should not be considered as reason for disability in matters pertaining to the enjoyment of civil and political rights." The fact that the treaty provisions were flagrantly violated by Rumania, under the pretext that the Jews were without rights not by reason of "differences of religious belief" but because they were aliens, does not diminish the accomplishment of the Alliance, for its work contributed some deposit to the foundation of the principle that human rights are a matter of international, and not purely domestic, concern.

Although the Alliance's central committee was located in Paris, the majority of its members were not French, and local and territorial committees of the Alliance existed in other countries. To this extent the organization was true to its original conception of being representative of universal Jewry and not merely of the Jews of France. But the leadership and control were mainly in the hands of French Jews; the opinions of others were welcome only as those of corresponding members. The time came when the German Jews felt that they had had enough of this treatment as second-class citizens, and so, in 1901, they formed their own organization, the Hilfsverein der deutschen Juden. Its purpose, too, was to improve the social and political conditions of their co-religionists in Eastern Europe and in the Orient. The Verein assisted in the emigration of Jews from Rumania and in the relief of Russian Jewry, and aided even in the self-defense measures of the Bund and the Zionists.

Even earlier, the English Jews were irritated by the superior attitude of the Parisian leaders of the Alliance, with the result that in 1871—only eleven years after the founding of the Alliance—they established the Anglo-Jewish Association, patterned after the Alliance but, like the Verein, not claiming or pretending to be representative of universal Jewry. It, too, was interested in establishing schools, and resorted to diplomacy on behalf of threatened or persecuted Jewish communities.

Beginning in 1881, however, the Anglo-Jewish Association cooperated with the Board of Deputies of British Jews, an organization founded in 1760. The year 1881 was a time of bloody pogroms in Russia when it was felt that British Jewry could not afford division; from then on, the Anglo-Jewish Association and the Board of Deputies acted on behalf of persecuted Jewish communities through a Joint Foreign Committee.

Here we should make mention of the work of Sir Moses Montefiore, whose diplomatic missions on behalf of stricken Jewish communities set the pattern for the Alliance, the Hilfsverein, and the Joint Foreign Committee. From the time of the notorious Damascus affair in 1840, he was intimately—and universally—identified with humanitarian efforts on behalf of his fellow Jews. He visited Russia in 1846 in support of Russian Jews, and went to Morocco in 1863 and to Rumania in 1867 on similar missions. In 1860 he went to Rome in connection with the *Mortara* case. The British government gave him its support, and everywhere it was known that he enjoyed the high personal regard of Queen Victoria. Although the Alliance did not succeed in becoming the voice of universal Jewry, Sir Moses Montefiore, by himself, achieved this status, for wherever he went, leaders of states and governments treated him as if he carried in his portfolio credentials, not only from the British government, but also from the Jewries of all Europe. Montefiore personified diplomacy as international intervention on behalf of human rights claimed by Jews; and though historians may question the degree of his success, all are in agreement that he fulfilled his function with great dignity, and that he accomplished the recognition of and brought honor to the idea of the humanitarian mission.

Just as the *Mortara* case shocked French Jewry into forming the Alliance, so, too, the American Jewish community—numbering then only 100,000—found themselves compelled to unite into the Board of Delegates of American Israelites, for the defense of Jewish rights and overseas relief; but it had only a feeble existence, and in 1878, when the Union of American Hebrew Congregations was formed, the Board became the Union's Board of Delegates on Civil and Religious Rights, but the change failed to enhance its effectiveness.

Then came to American Jews the waves of shock generated by the pogroms of 1903. There were protest meetings, and American Jews sent relief funds. Two years later came a second massacre at Kishinev, and in December of the same year, as soon as the czar's government put down the workers' insurrection in Moscow and quelled disorders, the autocratic regime was restored, and the concessions the czar had granted in October were almost wholly withdrawn, and fear replaced hope.

These events happened only four or five years after world Jewry had been stunned by the disclosure that Captain Alfred Dreyfus had been convicted on the basis of forged evidence—and this had happened, not in dark Russia, but in enlightened France!

The pain suffered by Jews everywhere in the world was deep and excruciating. American Jews could no longer remain satisfied with merely an occasional palliative offered to their less fortunate brethren. In 1906, under the leadership of Louis Marshall, Mayer Sulzberger, Jacob Schiff, Cyrus Adler, and Oscar Straus, the American Jewish Committee was formed

> to prevent the infraction of civil and religious rights of Jews, in any part of the world; to render all lawful assistance and to take appropriate remedial action in the event of threatened or actual invasion or destruction of such rights, or of unfavorable discrimination with respect thereto; to alleviate the consequences of persecution and to afford relief from calamities affecting Jews, wherever they may occur.[10]

It is significant that the American Jewish Committee, like its predecessors in England, Germany, and France, was created not to meet domestic needs, domestic anti-Semitism and discrimination, but to struggle on behalf of Jews harassed and persecuted in other countries. Each of the organizations was, at its inception, an association for international action on behalf of human rights for Jews.

There were problems everywhere. In England, Baron Lionel de Rothschild was elected to Parliament in 1847, but it was not until 1858 that he was allowed to take his seat as the first Jewish member of Parliament. It was not until 1870 that the legal difficulties were removed so that a Jew could become a scholar or a fellow in an English university. Indeed, it was not until 1890 that Jews had won complete political equality. In France, as the *Dreyfus* case made clear, anti-Semitism had deep roots and prevailed in almost every class and almost every aspect of French life and politics. The Jews of France were held responsible for nearly every wrong and crime. In Germany, despite constitutional guarantees, Jews were not appointed to government positions; they could not become army officers; they could not become full professors; and while German Jewry prospered, Jews lived under the dark shadow of anti-Semitism. In the United States, there was discrimination in housing, in educational opportunities, in employment—especially in banking, insurance, heavy industry; there was the suspicion of the Jew in populist tradition; there was the anti-Semitism of the nativist; there were the remnants of the Know-Nothing movement, and there was the Klu Klux Klan; there was the hatred of the immigrant and the foreigner. Yet, despite the problems and threats that the Jews faced at home, their dominant compulsion, their primary concern, was to try to save their fellow Jews who faced greater threats, a graver future. It was only the Russian Jews, as we have seen, who made the attempt to organize themselves for the struggle for their own civil rights and equality; their situation was so desperate that they were compelled to think of themselves, and only of themselves. Elsewhere, Jews organized not for themselves but on behalf of other Jews.

III

While devoting its best efforts and the largest part of its resources to helping persecuted Jews abroad, the American Jewish Committee encompassed in its program also the eradication of anti-Semitism and anti-Jewish discrimination at home.

In 1911, the American Jewish Committee amended its

charter to clarify its objective "to secure for Jews equality of economic, social and educational opportunity." In some instances, it was difficult to see a clear line between work on behalf of Jews abroad and work on behalf of one's own interests at home, as, for example, in the campaign for abrogation of the Russo-American treaty of 1832. Czarist Russia had imposed degrading and onerous restrictions on its Jewish subjects and also on American Jews visiting Russia. The Committee carried on a campaign to compel Russia to end this discrimination or to abrogate the treaty. In 1911 the treaty was abrogated. But the Committee's purpose in seeking this result was primarily to compel Russia to end its persecution of its own Jews, for only twenty-eight American Jews lived in Russia.[11] Thus, too, the Committee struggled for years to get Congress to repeal the odious immigration quota laws, which, by implication, branded East European Jews, and thus millions of American Jews, as undesirable.

Much of the work of the Committee, however, was clearly, without ambivalence, directed to a fight against the enemies at home. It fought against Henry Ford and his infamous *Dearborn Independent* and other anti-Semitic propaganda; it fought against the nativist Nazis and Fascists. It supported civil rights legislation with respect to places of public accommodation, and it promoted fair-employment and fair-educational-practices legislation, and it supported litigation attacking the restrictive covenant in housing. In all its efforts on the domestic front, the rationale of the Committee was that what was hurtful or degrading to American Jews, was hurtful or degrading to Americans. Thus, for example, when the Committee called on the United States government to do all it could to remove the humiliating disabilities from American Jews living in Russia, Louis Marshall formulated the Committee's rationale in these terms:

It is not the Jew who is insulted; it is the American people. And the finding of a proper remedy against this degradation is not a Jewish but an American question. . . . I should deplore the day when there should ever arise a Jewish, a Catholic or Protestant question in the United States. We can never suffer any question here concerning individual rights but such as relates to the entire American people.[12]

So, too, "when AJC mounted a successful campaign to prohibit discrimination in places of public accommodation in 1913, it was motivated by resort hotel advertisements stating that Jews were unwelcome; the corrective legislation was 'urged in the interest of the equality of all citizens before the law.'"[13] In defending the rights of Jews, then, the Committee was only defending the rights of all Americans. If the rights of American Jews were respected and were adequately protected by law, then, of course, all Americans would also benefit.

The primary, indeed, the exclusive, concern was with the rights of American Jews, for the Committee refused to get involved where the beneficiaries of social action would be only some other group. For example, when in the administration of Woodrow Wilson, blacks were displaced from government service or were subjected to a rigid system of racial segregation, the Committee refused to get involved.[14] The Committee obviously looked at the American scene, not with the eyes of an undifferentiated American, but with the eyes of a Jew. It saw itself as an organization whose purpose was to defend the rights of Jews abroad and at home.

After World War II, however, the Committee's posture was radically changed. It moved from the defense of Jewish rights, rationalized as the rights of all Americans, to a candid program of the defense of human rights at home and abroad. The argument had been turned around: instead of thinking that when the rights of Jews were vindicated, the rights of all Americans were also vindicated, now the thought was that since human rights include the rights of Jews, the Committee was justified when it worked directly for human rights. In 1947 the Committee agreed to support the campaign of the National Association for the Advancement of Colored People (NAACP) for an antilynching federal law, though the only instance of a Jew in the United States ever having been lynched was that of Leo Frank in Georgia in 1913.[15] The executive committee adopted a resolution that pledged the Committee's support of causes not specifically Jewish:

> It is resolved that the Executive Committee recognizes that there is the closest relation between the protection of the civil rights of all citizens and the protection of the civil rights of the members of particular groups; that it is a proper exercise of the powers of our Charter that the American Jewish Committee join with other groups in the protection of the civil rights of the members of all groups irrespective of race, religion, color or national origin; and that it is our general policy so to do."[16]

From a Jewish defense agency, primarily concerned with defense of Jews in Russia and in the Ottoman Empire, the American Jewish Committee had moved to becoming a general Jewish defense agency, concerned with Jewish rights at home and abroad, and then, in the 1940's, to becoming a general social-action and civil rights-civil liberties organization—without in the least losing or compromising its Jewish character, its vigilance as a Jewish defense agency, its Jewish motivation, and its Jewish idealism.

The other Jewish defense organizations in the United States —the American Jewish Congress, which became a permanent body in 1918–1922, and the Jewish Labor Committee, established in 1934—followed essentially the pattern set by the American Jewish Committee, which, from the time of its founding, never lost its drive. But the organizations differed in their constituencies, in their styles of life and action, and in their emphases.

But it may be that, in one very important respect, it was the American Jewish Congress that set the pattern and the pace, and that the Committee got its cue from the Congress. For directly after World War II, in 1945, the American Jewish Congress adopted a new program for Jewish action that had been prepared for it by the late Alexander H. Pekelis, in a paper that projected and charted a new program and formulated its underlying philosophy.

Pekelis took as his foundation stones two basic ideas, one of them from the Russian Jews who emphasized the need for Jewish self-determination and Jewish group autonomy, and the other from the American idea of cultural pluralism, of which Horace M. Kallen was the leading proponent, and on these foundations built the program for Jewish action toward full equality in a free society.[17] This program was intended to assure that individual freedom was coupled with group expression. Individuals must be allowed the basic rights with which God endowed them, but at the same time the historical reality must be recognized that individuals share a common group existence and group destiny. There must be individual freedom, and also group autonomy; American society is committed to both individualism *and* pluralism. The Constitution guarantees to minorities the right to preserve their minority characteristics; and because the United States is, in a sense, a multinational state, it cherishes both individual equality and group distinctiveness.

With these values or ideals as background, Pekelis sketched five major fields of action:

First, concern for Jewish equality at home, equality in law, and equality in fact;

Second, protection of our civil liberties from the violent and fraudulent manipulations of neofascists and anti-Semites;

Third, active alliance with all progressive and minority groups engaged in the building of a better America;

Fourth, participation in the [American Jewish] Congress's attempt to protect the lives and secure the rights of what remains of the Jews all over the world; and

Last, but not least, action within the Jewish community aimed at communal self-knowledge, communal self-control, and communal revival.

The essentially new ingredients were the third and fifth objectives. The third item, which is our present concern, called for the building of a better America, with the Jewish groups working in the vanguard for social progress, *whether or not the individual issues involved touch directly upon so-called Jewish interests.*[18]

It was natural that Jewish settlers in America should seek companionship and a sense of security by joining fraternal orders; besides, as de Tocqueville had observed in 1835, Americans tended to be a nation of joiners. Thus by 1860 there were already five Jewish fraternal orders.[19] Among them, B'nai B'rith, founded in 1843, grew most rapidly. Its members began to project purposes that transcended mere "togetherness," mutual aid, and insurance; by 1868 B'nai B'rith emphasized a program of philanthropy and political action for the protection of Jewish rights in the United States and abroad. Before the end of the century it had established cooperative relations with the Alliance Israélite Universelle, with whom it intervened against a treaty with Switzerland that discriminated against American Jews.[20] In important respects B'nai B'rith was a forerunner of the American Jewish Committee and of the American Jewish Congress; indeed, when the Committee was formed in 1906, it was apparent to the founders and to B'nai B'rith that their interests overlapped and that there was room for cooperation between the two organizations.[21] In 1913 B'nai B'rith organized its Anti-Defamation League. The League's charter stated that though "the immediate object of the League is to stop . . . the defamation of the Jewish people," the League's "ultimate purpose is to secure justice and fair treatment to *all citizens alike* and to put an end forever to unjust discrimination against *any sect or body of citizens*."[22]

It is apparent that all three organizations—the American Jewish Committee, the American Jewish Congress, and the Anti-Defamation League—went through the same stages of development. They began with a concern for Jews who needed help in other parts of the world. They then added the struggle against anti-Semitism in the United States and a concern with winning civil rights for all Americans without regard to creed or race. They are the least parochial of America's civil rights groups. International and transsectarian concerns are built in. And their records show that they have been faithful in pursuing these concerns. The Anti-Defamation League, like the other two organizations, also has had an interest in the sponsorship of social research. Its fact-gathering and reporting interests have resulted in publication of many notable volumes.

In response to a danger signal in any field of action, lay and professional troubleshooters from the different Jewish agencies are called to the scene at once. The need for cooperation has always been apparent. To meet this need, in 1944 the National Jewish Community Relations Advisory Council came into being by resolution of the General Assembly of the Council of Jewish Federations and Welfare Funds. In addition to the Congress, the Committee, and the League, the Council comprises the Jewish Labor Committee, the Jewish War Veterans, the National Council of Jewish Women, and three leading lay religious groups: The Union of American [Reform] Hebrew Congregations, the Union of Orthodox Jewish Congregations, and the United [Conservative] Synagogue of America. Over eighty local Jewish community relations councils are also members. Thus the Council is a widely representative organization. It stands solidly and militantly for a civil rights program that embraces all minorities as its beneficiaries, without regard to religion or race.

To a greater or lesser degree, all American Jewish defense organizations, but especially the Committee and Congress, have adopted the Pekelis program, and are seriously dedicated to each of its five objectives. They remain Jewish defense agencies, and yet at the same time each is a league for the promotion and protection of fundamental human rights, without regard to whether the issues over these rights affect directly Jewish interests.

This, one may say, is a unique American Jewish contribution, for it brings to a single focus the philosophy of cultural pluralism, the ideals of the Hebrew prophets, the promises of the Declaration of Independence, and the philosophy of the Bill of Rights of the United States Constitution.

7 /

Life and Liberty
for the Pursuit of Happiness

We hold these truths to be self-evident, that all
men are created equal, that they are endowed by
their Creator with certain unalienable Rights, that
among these are Life, Liberty, and the pursuit of Happiness.

IF I WERE TOLD that one day in the distant future
our civilization would crumble into dust, as was the fate of
many ancient civilizations that are presently the objects of
archaeological study, but that I now had the opportunity and
privilege to select a single short text that would be preserved
and read as our legacy to future mankind as the mark of our
ideals and aspirations, I think that I would choose this single
sentence from the Declaration of Independence. And I venture
that most Americans would agree and would believe with me
that, indeed, there could be no other choice.

I

Most of the Declaration of Independence is given over
to an indictment of George III and of the British policies toward

the American colonies, and the philosophical statement is only a short paragraph. For its time and occasion, the charge against the British was by far the more important, but once the Revolution was successfully accomplished, the indictment of the British government took on only a topical and historical interest, while the philosophical paragraph became the heart of the document and America's most sacred text. When Jefferson, toward the end of his life, considered the Declaration of Independence, he wrote to Madison that he himself valued his statement of principles more than his indictment of British policy,[1] and posterity has handsomely confirmed Jefferson's judgment.

But, interestingly, there is nothing in this part of the document that is original with Jefferson or with his American contemporaries. Its ideas have been traced by scholars, time and again, to Greek political thought, to Locke, Hutcheson, Priestley, Burlamaqui, Bolingbroke;[2] to Wollaston, Adam Smith, Hume, Lord Kames, Blackstone, Hobbes, Beccaria, Oliver Goldsmith, and Dr. Johnson.[3] "The truth is," wrote Carl Becker in his magisterial fashion, "that the philosophy of Nature, in its broader aspects and in its particular applications, was thoroughly English. English literature of the seventeenth and eighteenth centuries is steeped in this philosophy. The Americans did not borrow it, they inherited it. The lineage is direct: Jefferson copied Locke and Locke quoted Hooker."[4]

Yet its lack of fundamental originality was not a defect but a virtue. Jefferson had only seventeen days in which to carry out his assignment from the Continental Congress, and he turned to neither book nor pamphlet for ideas or phrases. "I did not," he wrote later, "consider it as any part of my charge to invent new ideas altogether and to offer no sentiment which had never been expressed before."[5] In a letter he wrote a year before his death, Jefferson stated why he had not sought originality and what it was that he had sought to express:

Not to find out new principles, or new arguments, never before thought of, not merely to say things which had never been said before; but to place before mankind the common sense of the subject, in terms so plain and firm as to command their assent, and to justify ourselves in the independent stand we are compelled to take. Neither aiming at originality of principle or sentiment, nor yet copied from any particular and previous writing, it was intended to be an expression of the American mind, and to give to that expression the proper tone and spirit called for by the occasion. All its authority rests on the harmonizing sentiments of the day, whether expressed in conversation, in letters, printed essays, on the elementary books of public right, as Aristotle, Cicero, Locke, Sidney, etc.[6]

Jefferson was, of course, quite right in the way he saw his assignment: it was not to frame a personal statement, which would bear his name, as author, but to express the thoughts and convictions, the sentiments and beliefs of the men who would sign it and thereby become the proclaimers and leaders of the American Revolution. He therefore sought to express "the American mind" and "the common sense of the subject." In the Declaration, Jefferson was the voice of the American people.

It is precisely this quality that makes the Declaration a unique document in world history, for never before had a *nation* subscribed to the belief that all men are created equal; that all men are endowed by God with certain inalienable rights; that all men have the inalienable right to life, liberty, and the pursuit of happiness; never before had a nation subscribed to these beliefs except ancient Israel. Jefferson copied Locke, and Locke quoted Hooker, and Hooker copied Thomas Aquinas, and Thomas Aquinas transmitted the teachings of Aristotle and the Bible.

On June 12, 1776, only a few weeks before the Continental Congress approved the Declaration of Independence, the Virginia Assembly adopted the Virginia Bill of Rights, written by George Mason. The first of the articles of the Virginia Bill of Rights read as follows: "That all men are by nature equally free and independent, and have certain inherent rights, of which, when they enter into a state of society, they cannot, by any compact, deprive their posterity; namely, the enjoyment of life and liberty, with the means of acquiring and possessing property, and pursuing and obtaining happiness and safety."[7] The similarity, and in some respects even the identity, of language is striking. Did Jefferson plagiarize George Mason? We have Jefferson's own word that he had no books or documents from which to copy, and that what he sought was to express "the American mind." What Jefferson wrote was good Locke, good George Mason, just as what Mason wrote was good Locke, good Jefferson; for what they wrote was the common doctrine of Virginians, the common doctrine of Americans, the common doctrine of the times.[8] And again I say that it is precisely in this that one finds the greatness of Jefferson's achievement.

The amiable and witty Sydney Smith, when confronted with Macaulay's fabulous memory, remarked that Macaulay would be well-advised to take two tablespoonfuls of the waters of Lethe every morning, so that his retentive powers would be contracted.[9] Fortunately for the world, Jefferson, as he prepared the Declaration of Independence, seems to have followed (though Macaulay unfortunately did not) Sydney Smith's excellent prescription. The literary critic, Harold Bloom, in his book *Poetry and Repression* (1976), wrote: "If any poet knows too well what causes his poem, then he cannot write it, or at least will write it badly. He must repress the causes, including the precursor poems." Wisely, as he himself knew, and as we know, Jefferson, when faced by his colossal task, repressed his memories of Algernon Sidney, John Locke, Harrington, and a whole library of books in philosophy and political theory and history, so that what he wrote is pure, or almost pure, Jefferson. He had every right to ask that on his tombstone there be inscribed the following epitaph: "Here was buried Thomas Jefferson, author of the Declaration of American Independence, of the statute of Virginia for religious freedom, and father of the University of Virginia."

An aspect of Jefferson's achievement that especially arrests attention is his use of the phrase "the pursuit of happiness." Locke's phrase was life, liberty, and property; or the "lives, liberties, and estates," which he called "by the general name, property";[10] or "lives, liberties and fortunes."[11] The substitution of "the pursuit of happiness" for "property" involved a leap of the imagination and mind which, after the lapse of two centuries, still seems staggering. How did it happen?

We would give much to know, but Jefferson never explained, and it may well be that he did not himself know how to account for it; for the mind is a subtle thing, and it does not always disclose its secrets. Will we ever know how Keats came to write that "beauty is truth, truth beauty"? Did Keats himself ever know?[12]

Jefferson, himself a property owner and an agrarian,[13] was no enemy of private property.[14] It may well be that, as he was drafting the Declaration, he had in mind a distinction between natural rights and civil rights, a distinction made or intimated by Christian Wolff, Blackstone, and Burlamaqui.[15] This distinction is one that he shared with Thomas Paine and may even have suggested to Paine, who illustrated the distinction in the following way: Suppose, wrote Paine, that twenty persons, strangers to one another, meet in an uninhabited country. "Each would be a sovereign in his own natural right." Each person's will would be his own law, but his power would be threatened by the power of the other nineteen persons. It would then occur to them that their condition would be improved if they could devise a way to convert their danger into protection, so that each would be protected by the other nineteen inhabitants. Thinking this through, they are bound to see that there is a distinction between rights which they could exercise without the help of others, and rights which they could not enjoy unless protected by others.

Of the first kind are the rights of thinking, speaking, forming and giving opinions, and perhaps all those which can be fully exercised by the individual without the aid of exterior assistance—or in other words, rights of personal competency—Of the second kind are those of personal protection of acquiring and possessing property, in the exercise of which the individual natural power is less than the natural right.[16]

The latter rights Paine called civil rights "or rights of Compact," that is, rights that are contingent upon the existence of a social contract. They are, he wrote, distinguishable from natural rights "because in the one [in the case of natural rights] we act wholly in our own person, in the other [the civil rights] we agree not to do so, but act under the guarantee of society."

From this analysis it would follow that the rights of property are only "imperfect natural rights," for individuals lack the power adequately to protect themselves in the possession and enjoyment of property. While one can think, speak, and form one's opinions without the support of others, one cannot claim the ownership of property without such outside support.

At first blush it may seem strange that religious liberty was not associated with freedom of thought and freedom of speech as one of the "perfect natural rights," but perhaps Jefferson and Paine excluded religious liberty from this category because they saw that the exercise of religious liberty entailed a place of worship, publication of sacred books, and schools for religious instruction—all of them activities that were dependent upon the ownership of property: of a church, chapel, or synagogue, a printing press, and school facilities. Without access to such resources, freedom of religion could mean only the freedom to think and speak. All we need to do is to think of religion in the Soviet Union since the Bolshevik Revolution to see how dependent religious liberty is on the guarantee of the rights of private property; but Jefferson and Paine could easily have thought of examples nearer to them in time and space—the condition of Protestants in Catholic countries, or the condition of dissenters in England or of nonconformists in an American colony that had an established church. It thus must have been apparent to them that religious liberty was an "imperfect natural right," because its meaningful exercise could take place only "under the guarantee of society."

Indeed, a critical analysis of freedom of speech would, I think, lead to the conclusion that it, too, can be exercised only "under the guarantee of society," for we have seen many cases where a small number of militant leftists or rightists have effectively prevented a person from speaking and his audience from hearing him. When a speaker does not have the protection of society, his freedom of speech becomes patently an "imperfect natural right." Thomas Paine and Thomas Jefferson could have talked eloquently about this from what they had themselves observed of the actions of mobs and mobsters.

In a letter to Colonel David Humphreys, Jefferson wrote that there are rights that one cannot surrender, and yet they are rights that governments have always sought to invade. "These are," he wrote, "the rights of thinking, and publishing our thoughts by speaking or writing; the right of free commerce [travel]; the right of personal freedom [probably what today we would call the right of privacy]."[17] Since this letter was written by Jefferson from Paris in March 1789, before Congress adopted the Bill of Rights of the United States Constitution,[18] he went on to urge the framing and adoption of such an instrument, which should include, he said, the right to trial by jury. Now, obviously such a right cannot exist except in so far is it is guaranteed by society. Earlier, in December 1787, he wrote to Madison from Paris that he liked the Constitution proposed by the Convention, but then went on to say:

I will now add what I do not like. First the omission of a Bill of Rights providing clearly and without the aid of sophisms for freedom of religion, freedom of the press, protection against standing armies, restriction against monopolies, the eternal and unremitting force of the habeas corpus laws, and trials by jury in all matters of fact. . . . Let me add that a bill of rights is what the people are entitled to against every government on earth, general or particular, and what no just government should refuse.[19]

It is significant, I think, that in this letter, one of the most important that he ever wrote, the one essential freedom that he does *not* mention among those enumerated for inclusion in a bill of rights is freedom of speech. All the freedoms he enumerates are such as are significant only if guaranteed and supported by government. One may assume that he thought that freedom of speech is, indeed, a "pure natural right," for the exercise of which no government support or constitutional guarantee was necessary. As we have seen, he was wrong in this, and fortunately Madison, when he framed the Bill of Rights, rode above the deep waters of theory and wisely wrote into the First Amendment the guarantee of freedom of speech, as well as guarantees of freedom of press, religion, and assembly.

In this matter Madison stayed closer to Locke than did Jefferson, for Locke made no distinction between pure and impure natural rights, and maintained that when men left the state of nature and made a social contract and instituted government, the government had no power to destroy but had only the power to preserve the rights which men would have if they lived in a state of nature. Men do not leave their natural rights behind but take them with them into civil society. "The obligations of the law of nature," wrote Locke, "cease not in [civil] society . . . the law of nature stands as an eternal rule to all men, legislators [i.e., the government] as well as others. The rules that they [i.e., the legislators] make for other men's actions must, as well as their own and other men's action, be conformable to the law of nature, *i.e.*, to the will of God, of which that is a declaration."[20]

In another respect, however, it was fortunate that Jefferson did not try simply to echo Locke's words. His most daring and significant innovation was to substitute "the pursuit of happiness" for "property." Yet here again we are compelled to enter a qualification, for the innovation was not an absolute one. While Locke makes no mention of the pursuit of happiness in his *Second Treatise*, he does use the phrase several times in *An Essay Concerning Human Understanding*.[21] There is, for example, this phrase that may be cited: "Thus, how much soever men are in earnest and constant in pursuit of happiness. . . ."[22] And, as we have noted, the phrase "pursuit of happiness" can be found in other writings that were probably familiar to Jefferson, but his use of it in collocation with "life" and "liberty" elevated the idea to a supreme value. In the context of the Declaration of Independence, the phrase loses its character as a mere psychological description of what men may desire. It becomes a moral end and makes a revolutionary claim on political institutions. From a report about consciousness it becomes a moral and political imperative. One familiar with the political and philosophical literature against which Jefferson's document may be read recognizes the phrase "the pursuit of happiness," and is struck by the "shock of recognition."[23]

II

The explosive vitality of the Jeffersonian phrase projected it into the future, as a promise of a new perspective, a new vision, a new life. It was a symbol marking a break with the past, and a maxim to lead the American revolutionaries into their promised land.

For beginning with the Renaissance and during the two hundred years preceding 1776, men slowly drifted away from the Christian obsession with other-worldliness, asceticism, austerity, and self-mortification. People questioned a moral order that idealized poverty and celibacy, that placed an almost impregnable wall between matter and spirit, between body and soul, between earth and heaven, between this life and the life to come. People muttered against and resented a social order in which happiness was reserved for a small, select body of nobles and aristocrats, while millions of men, women, and children could only look to a life of misery, hunger, and sickness.

The discovery of new lands, the invention of new machines, and the extension of the idea of the division of labor brought about great changes in commerce and industry which gradually but firmly superimposed upon the Christian other-worldly ideals a strong desire for and movement toward material prosperity. In place of an economy of scarcity, people had begun to look for an economy of plenty. In place of a society rigidly structured on tiers of social classes, people talked of equality; they dared to think and sometimes even to say that all are created equal. In place of obedience and subjection, in a social order that had a place for slavery, serfdom, and bondage, people talked of liberty. In place of duty, they spoke of rights. In place of sorrow, discontent, and misery, they spoke of happiness and of the pursuit of happiness.

One could cite many examples of this new spirit that was agitating society, but I will choose only two. The first example is Erasmus's *In Praise of Folly*, which, published in 1511, at once captivated all Europe. Through the disguises assumed by the author, the reader could easily get the message, which was that it was good to take pleasure from life and stupid to make a virtue out of misery. Through the book, readers were compelled to face the fact that the Creator had so fashioned the world that life could not go on if men did not find happiness in women and if women, despite the trouble and pain, did not find happiness in their husbands and children. Erasmus, through the mouth of Folly, argued that, contrary to what people had been taught for centuries, self-love was essential to happiness, for what man, asked Folly, could give pleasure to others if he gave no pleasure to himself? Said Erasmus, I could love my neighbor as myself, as the Bible teaches me, only if I first loved myself. Some of his sharpest barbs are directed at theologians and priests, who multiply distinctions and useless definitions, play with abstract questions and preach absurd ethical rules, and rely on fantasy to create their own pictures of heaven and hell; they preach what is absurd and keep up only the forms of religion, while the simple teachings of Christianity are neglected or, worse, are made to appear foolish or even criminal.

The second example I would offer is Mandeville's famous *Fable of the Bees*, published two centuries later, in 1714, a book that has been of great importance both for those who, like the later utilitarians, were influenced by its doctrines, and those who challenged and attacked its premises and conclusions. The book's importance to us is that it marks a clean break with the moral assumptions and teachings of the past centuries. The book's central message was that if Englishmen desired material prosperity, then the way to its achievement was not through the Christian, medieval path of self-denial, but through the expression of self-interest—yes, through the traditional "vices" of pride, vanity, and self-seeking. It was these so-called vices, Mandeville contended, that could account for the elementary comforts that commerce and industry had provided. Without human desire, and its legitimation, progress toward wealth or civilization was impossible. It follows that religious or legal restraints on the commercial and industrial pursuits which seek the satisfaction of material wants are unnatural, for they prevent progress and prosperity.

Now, what could better summarize and project this new philosophy than the phrase "life, liberty, and the pursuit of happiness"? In its starkness and shrillness, it first of all was a protest against and a rejection of the traditional conception of society in which common people had no claim on the attainment of property, status, and privilege; and it was, secondly, a promise of a new order, in which government was to be the agent of all the people and help them in their efforts to win for themselves a measure of human, earthly happiness.

The spirit of this quality of Jefferson's phrase was beautifully expressed by Leonard Woolf almost fifty years before the American Bicentennial:

When the democrats proclaimed that everyone had socially an equal and "inalienable right to the pursuit of happiness," they laid the foundations for one of the greatest social, political, and psychological revolutions that the world has known. Happiness, it is generally agreed, depends on the enjoyment of both material and mental things. An adequate income, a nice house, pleasant things to eat and drink, fine clothes, a barouche and spinet in one generation or a motor-car and gramophone in another, a garden, travel, leisure, and conversation, a university education, an interesting profession, the ability to understand and therefore the opportunity to enjoy a poem of Donne or a Quartet of Beethoven—these are the things which the profoundest philosophers and the most acute thinkers and observers agree are important ingredients in human happiness. Today there are millions of people in the world who instinctively, unconsciously believe that none of these ingredients of happiness are by right the particular property of particular persons or classes. Writers on democracy have not paid sufficient attention to the fact that before the nineteenth [he should have said the eighteenth] century at no period of the world's history did anyone believe any such thing; that on the contrary everyone [he should have said nearly everyone] believed the exact opposite; and that this revolution in communal psychology can be traced to the fundamental proposition in the American Declaration of Independence, and so to the fundamental doctrine of modern democracy.[24]

III

Our discussion should, I believe, have made it clear that Jefferson's phrase historically has served two functions: first, it encapsulates complex economic, political, religious, and social developments that ran their course from the Renaissance to the American Revolution, and secondly, it projects for the future centuries, from 1776 onward into our own day and beyond, economic, political, religious, and social forces that make the happiness of all people—or, to use the more fashionable term, social progress or social welfare—the prime end of the social contract.

The pursuit of happiness has been and continues as a fundamental motive force that propels states and peoples throughout the world to develop their agriculture, to exploit their natural and human resources, to industrialize, to spread literacy and education, to engage in slum-clearance and public-housing projects, to be interested in public sanitation and the construction of hospitals, to struggle against poverty and sickness, to end unemployment and economic exploitation or deprivation. No constitution, no bill of rights in the world today proclaims that it is better to be poor than rich, better to suffer than to enjoy life, better to endure misery than to find remedies for social afflictions, better to seek an economy of scarcity than an economy of affluence and plenty.[25]

Matthew Arnold—or any person, for that matter—may set for himself as his goal or way of life the pursuit of perfection; Spinoza may set for himself the pursuit of salvation or blessedness; Kant may set for himself a life devoted to the pursuit of duty. What a *person* chooses for himself is his own affair. But a *society* today cannot make such subjective choices. Adelbert Stifter, at the end of a despairing letter to his publisher and friend, wrote: "I do not want to have my suffering taken from me, for that would be to take the divine from me as well." We can sense and respect the great nobility of such a sentiment. But no government could last a day if it proclaimed that it would dedicate its energies and power to the perpetuation of suffering so that human beings may retain their divinity.

"Happiness," Lord David Cecil has written, "must come unsought in this hard world: pursued, it eludes us."[26] This may be true for the individual, for whom happiness may be a subtle mood, a delicate state of being in which, as Socrates would say, the outer and inner man are at one, a state of being in which the mind and heart find themselves wonderfully in balance.[27] Society, however, cannot sit back and wait for the welfare of its members to come from heaven. In this hard world, society must seek its welfare just as it seeks its safety or security.

But I venture to suggest that from the standpoint of Judaism, when it clings to its roots in the Hebrew Scriptures, even for the individual there is the task of actively seeking and pursuing happiness. Just as there is the happiness of duty, so, too, there is the duty of happiness. When the pilgrim brought to the priest his first fruit in a basket, the priest was to receive the basket and place it before the altar, and the Israelite was to prostrate himself before the Lord and say: "And now, behold, I have brought the first of the fruit of the land, which Thou, O Lord, has given me." And then the text says: "And thou shalt rejoice in all the good which the Lord thy God hath given unto thee, and unto thy house."[28] Indeed, one of the reasons for the wrath of God is "because thou didst not serve the Lord thy God with joyfulness, and the gladness of heart, for the abundance of all things."[29] When the Israelite was to bring a tithe of his grain, his wine, and his oil, but was permitted to convert their value into money, he was to use the money "for whatsoever thy soul desireth, for oxen, or for sheep, or for wine, or for strong drink, or for whatsoever thy soul asketh of thee; and thou shalt eat there before the Lord thy God, and thou shalt rejoice, thou and thy household."[30] In Judaism there is the *Simcha shel Mitzvah*, the joy of the commandment, the happiness of duty, and there is also *the commandment to be joyful*, the *Mitzvah shel Simcha*, the duty of happiness.[31]

And when God addresses the community, the Bible clearly and explicitly makes the social blessing dependent upon society's fulfillment of the Lord's commandments. But the important point for us to note in the context of our discussion is that the blessing is defined in terms that we would today consider marks of social welfare or happiness. If the Israelites will keep the commandments, then the land will flow with milk and honey, the rains will come in season, the people will gather in their grain, their wine, and their oil; their cattle will be fed with the grass of the fields, the people will eat and be full.[32] "The Lord your God will make you abundantly prosperous in all the work of your hand, in the fruit of your body, and in the fruit of your cattle, and in the fruit of your ground; for the Lord will again take delight in prospering you, as he took delight in your fathers."[33] The Bible built no impregnable wall between the sacred and the secular, between matter and spirit, between body and soul, and so it has no hesitation in linking the commandments with prosperity, in linking *mitzvahs* with joy and pleasure, and in making an ineluctable connection between the pursuit of righteousness and the pursuit of happiness.

Judaism would not have survived all the catastrophes that the Jewish people have suffered over the millennia if the Jews did not have, at the core of their hearts, the sentiment, the instinct, the drive to face life with the conviction that life is worth living, that God's creation must be good, that it is sinful to be melancholic and misanthropic, that they must choose the blessing and life. Isaiah gave voice to this proclamation in favor of life and liberty for the pursuit of happiness:

But be ye glad and rejoice for ever
In that which I create;
For behold, I create Jerusalem a rejoicing,
And her people a joy.
And I will rejoice in Jerusalem,
And joy in my people;
And the voice of weeping shall be no more heard in her,
Nor the voice of crying.
There shall be no more thence an infant of days,
   nor an old man that hath not filled his days,
For the youngest shall die a hundred years old.

And they shall build houses and inhabit them;
And they shall plant vineyards and eat the fruit of them. . .
Behold, my servants shall drink. . .
Behold, my servants shall rejoice. . .
Behold, my servants shall sing
For joy of heart.[34]

Of course this is a promise, but it is also a program. But so was Jefferson's phrase. It was not a statement of what had already been achieved. It was a promise and a program.

While Christianity is undergoing a crisis in its attempt to meet the challenge of the new philosophy of happiness, which finds no virtue in miseries that human intelligence can prevent, Judaism is not faced with a similar crisis. For Judaism has never preached that the body is evil, that the earth is profane, that poverty is a blessing, that scarcity is better than plenty. Renunciation as a way of meeting life's problems is no part of Judaism, which has always affirmed life. Judaism has never put an abyss between good and evil, saint and sinner, the saved and the damned, the selfish virtues and the social virtues, body and soul, earth and heaven, the city of God and the city of man, revelation and intelligence, time and eternity, man and woman, religion and culture. Not escape from life but involvement in and the betterment of life has been the Jewish ideal. Insofar as the peoples of the world now accept this view, they accept at least part of the teaching that has come out of Zion.

Take, first of all, the plain fact of longevity. Throughout the Hebrew Scriptures we find a persistent emphasis on the desirability of a long span of years. Abraham "died in a good old age." I cannot recall a single Biblical hero who died young. For an event of this sort we have to turn to the New Testament. Jesus was only in his early thirties when he died; and he was the first Jew whose *death* was celebrated. In the Hebrew Scriptures the emphasis is always on life, not death. The essence of this Biblical affirmation of life is stated in Psalm 115: "May the

Lord increase you, you and your children. . . . The heavens are the heavens of the Lord; but the earth hath He given to the children of men. The dead praise not the Lord, neither any that go down into silence; but we [the living] will bless the Lord from this time forth and for evermore."

The body, whether of a man or a woman, is not, in Judaism, the creation of Satan. It is the creation of God, as Genesis teaches. The body is the gateway of life and a source of joy. Abraham is quoted as saying to Sarah: "I know that you are a woman beautiful to behold"; and Isaac knew that Rebecca his wife "was fair to look upon." The patriarchs did not close their eyes to the beauty of God's creatures. And there is the story of Jacob's long wooing of Rachel, not the *idea* of Rachel, but the real woman. Not to the scale of angels are the patriarchs drawn but as men of flesh and bone and spirit—whole persons as God made them.

"And thou shalt love the Lord thy God with all thy heart, and with all thy soul, and with all thy might." To the rabbis "with all thy heart" meant "with all thy desires, including the *yetzer hara*, the evil inclination." The Jew must make even his passions and ambitions contribute to the service of God. The "evil inclination" is not to be rooted out; it is to be made the servant, rather than the master, of the whole person. This point is put in daring language in the Midrash:

> "It was very good" (Genesis 1:31). Rabbi Nahman b. Samuel said: That is the evil inclination. But is the evil inclination very good? Yes, for if it were not for the evil inclination, man would not build a house, or take a wife, or beget a child, or engage in business, as it says, "All labor and skillful work comes of a man's rivalry with his neighbor."[35]

Everywhere in the Hebrew Scriptures "freedom from want," an economy of abundance is held up as a divine ideal for man. The Promised Land which the Lord conjures up for the Israelites is "a good land, a land of brooks of water, of fountains and depths, springing forth in valleys and hills; a land of wheat and barley, and vines and fig-trees and pomegranates; a land of olive trees and honey; a land wherein thou shalt eat bread without scarceness, thou shalt not lack anything in it. . . . And thou shalt eat and be satisfied." Job, the man of Uz who "was blameless and upright, one who feared God, and turned away from evil," had a wife and ten children, seven thousand sheep, three thousand camels, five hundred yoke of oxen, five hundred she-asses, and very many servants. He was a rich man, yet there is no intimation that Job could no more enter heaven than a camel could go through the eye of a needle.

The genius of Judaism resides not in reducing the sacred to the profane or secular, but in raising the secular to the sacred, the material to the spiritual. Just as Judaism raised the seventh day to the Sabbath, so it seeks to raise every weekday to the Sabbath; so that in the end the distinction would be not between the sacred and the secular, but between the sacred and the sacred (*ben kodesh le-kodesh*).

The ideal of Judaism is a kingdom of heaven on this earth in which every man will live under his own vine and his own fig tree, enjoying God's bounty, free from want and fear, in a social order based on justice, freedom, and righteousness: an order of society which combines God's bounty with God's law—man walking in the way which the Lord commanded him, and God prolonging man's days, and blessing the fruit of his body and the fruit of his land, a nation constituting a kingdom of priests, a holy people. Man is given dominion over nature, over the works of God's hands; all things have been put under his feet, "all sheep and oxen, and also the beasts of the field, the birds of the air and the fish of the sea, whatever passes along the paths of the sea." This is what it means to have been made "little less than divine" and to have been crowned with glory and honor.

"The ant is knowing and wise, but he doesn't know enough to take a vacation," Clarence Day said. "The worshiper of energy is too physically energetic to see that he cannot explore certain higher fields until he is still." But Judaism, with its emphasis on righteousness, with its institution of the Sabbath day, and with the importance it attaches to study as a form of worship, has taught the Jew to avoid imitation of the ant. The Jew has been taught to stand still. But a vacation is important only if one customarily works, and to stand still is important only if one is ordinarily in motion. Judaism tries to be true to a healthy rhythm of life. Built into it, therefore, is a principle of asceticism which is not that of total resignation or renunciation, but of acceptance of the vital needs of the whole human being, the needs of getting and spending, of work and rest, of affirmation and denial. The person must be engaged and yet suspended, involved and yet withdrawn. Judaism teaches self-denial for the sake of a greater affirmation. Jewish asceticism is, thus, one of the poles of a natural organic rhythm; it is an asceticism that affirms life and serves the self in its quest for fulfillment. It is not stagnation, not resignation, not renunciation, but the sabbatical pause, the sabbatical rest, the sabbatical withdrawal that is itself an enjoyment as man lets his soul loaf and looks for reconciliation with all that is beautiful and holy.

Some Christian theologians have begun to turn against the traditional Christian perversion of the Jewish attitude to life. Tillich, Reinhold Niebuhr, and Cherbonnier were among the leaders in this effort to reinterpret Christianity. For example, Cherbonnier's reinterpretation of the doctrine of sin in the light of Old Testament teaching led him to affirm the *goodness* of creation, and the radical freedom of man, and to call the doctrine of original sin and belief in predestination Christian misconceptions. In reaching this conclusion he found it necessary to challenge Augustine, Thomas Aquinas, Luther, and Calvin, in the name of and for the sake of Biblical religion. Insofar, he says, as Christianity manifests "a negative view of the world in general and a repressive attitude toward the flesh in particular," it has been infiltrated by "pagan value judgments." When Thomas Aquinas placed matter in the lower half of his scale of realities, he bifurcated human nature into mind and matter, and thereby sacrificed the Bible to Aristotle. And Cherbonnier goes on to say that the God of the Bible wants "not the annihilation of unruly passions, but their conversion, for the greatest power of evil may also be transformed into even greater forces for good." The Bible does not demand "*disuse* but redemption," and the "joyous affirmation of the goodness of the present life" is an essential Biblical outlook.[36]

Maimonides was aware that there were pious Jews who at times inclined to extremes by fasting, vigils, celibacy, wearing hair shirts, or by withdrawing to the mountains or desert, but Maimonides disapproved of such practices as a violation of the law, unless possibly resorted to as a form of therapy or as flight from corrupt society. The Torah, he said, mentions not a word in support of such extreme prescriptions. "The intention of the Law," Maimonides wrote,

is that men should live naturally and moderately, eating and drinking what he pleases in moderation, enjoying sexual unions as permitted, in moderation, living in society, uprightly and in good faith—not that he should live in mountain or desert wastes, wear hair shirts, or afflict his body. The admonition against such practices, according to the tradition, is in the statement that the Nazirite [i.e., a person who took an oath to be ascetic] "shall make atonement for himself for sinning against the soul" (Numbers 6:11). What soul did he sin against? ask the rabbis, of blessed memory. Against his own, by depriving himself of wine. Does it not follow *a fortiori* that if one who abstains from wine must make atonement, then one who deprives himself of all comfort and enjoyment must all the more so?[37]

IV

Writing in 1870, Emerson formulated a number of tests of civilization. First, he said, civilization depends upon man utilizing effectively the aid of nature, letting the elements do his hard work. That, he said, "is the wisdom of man, in every instance of his labor, to hitch his wagon to a star, and see his chore done by the gods themselves. That is the way we are strong, by borrowing the might of the elements."

Second, man, in his effort to become civilized, must lean on principles, for they are the most powerful of all supports. "Gibraltar may be strong," said Emerson, "but ideas are impregnable." Again, "Work . . . for those interests which the divinities honor and promote—justice, life, freedom, knowledge, utility."

Third, by working with the energies of the universe and the commandments of God, "we can harness also evil agents, the powers of darkness, and force them to serve against their will the ends of wisdom and virtue." The power "to combine antagonisms and utilize evil" is an index to civilization.[38]

In all this, Emerson, I submit, is describing not only civilization, but the genius of Judaism. He is giving expression to the hope that underlies the American dream: Hitch your wagon to a star, so that you may harness the star's energies to turn your wheels, so that the stars may do the work of innumerable human hands. Hitch your wagon to a star, so that you may raise your sights to the vision of celestial principles, which alone can make gods of all human beings—ideas like justice, truth, equality, freedom, goodness, beauty, happiness. Hitch your wagon to a star, so that you may harness the energies even of your "evil inclination" and let it, too, serve God.

This, as I know it, is the teaching of Judaism. It is also the sense of that glorious phrase of the Declaration of Independence: "life, liberty, and the pursuit of happiness."

True, the Biblical injunction is not: "Happiness, happiness shalt thou pursue." Israel was told: "Justice, justice shalt thou pursue." But as long as body and soul are conjoined, as long as the human being is a complex of matter and spirit, there can be no pursuit of justice without the pursuit of happiness. Humanity—since the eighteenth-century revolutions—has at last begun to accept this "word of the Lord out of Jerusalem."

NOTES

Notes to Introduction

1. Ralph Waldo Emerson, *English Traits* (1856), ed. Howard Mumford Jones (Cambridge, Mass., 1966), pp. 185–186. For the record of Emerson's journal entry, see *Journals and Miscellaneous Notebooks of Ralph Waldo Emerson (1847–1848)*, ed. M. M. Sealts, Jr. (Cambridge, Mass., 1973), X, 434.

2. Cf. Lincoln's phrase in the Gettysburg Address, November 19, 1863: "that government of the people, by the people, for the people, . . ."

3. Theodore Parker, *The Slave Power*, ed. James K. Hosmer (Centenary ed.; Boston, 1907), XI, 250. Parker speaks again of "the American idea" at p. 284. Cf. Horace M. Kallen, *Cultural Pluralism and the American Idea* (Philadelphia, 1956), p. 61, where reference is made to Parker's use of the phrase; and Everett Carter, *The American Idea: The Literary Response to American Optimism* (Chapel Hill, N.C., 1977), p. 7, where there is reference to Emerson's use of the term, and, p. 52, to James Russell Lowell's use of the term in a letter he wrote in December 1848.

4. E. B. White, *Essays* (New York, 1977), p. 60.

5. *Documents of American History*, ed. Henry Steele Commager (8th ed.; New York, 1968), p. 15.

6. "The Gods of the Nations and God," in Martin Buber, *Israel and the World* (New York, 1948), p. 198.

7. *Ibid.*, p. 197.

8. The Declaration of Independence, in Commager, *Documents of American History*, p. 100.

9. *Democratic Vistas* (1871), in *Walt Whitman*, ed. Mark Van Doren (Viking Portable Library ed.; New York, 1948), p. 390, italics supplied.

10. *Ibid.*, p. 393.

11. *Ibid.*, p. 397.

12. *Ibid.*, p. 400. This was written, it should be remembered, during the days of the notorious Grant administration.

13. *Ibid.*, pp. 416, 417.

14. *Ibid.*, p. 460.

15. *Ibid.*, p. 456.

16. *Ibid.*, p. 455.

17. *Ibid.*, p. 435.

18. *Ibid.*, pp. 448, 449.
19. *Ibid.*, pp. 453–454.
20. *Ibid.*, p. 469.
21. *The Portable Johnson and Boswell*, ed. Louis Kronenberger (New York, 1947), p. 111.
22. Deuteronomy 28:3–5.
23. *Ibid.*, 30:5.
24. Jeremiah 22:3, 5.
25. Deuteronomy 8:1, 3.
26. J. L. Tamon, "Reflections of an Historian in Jerusalem," *Encounter*, May 1976, p. 85.
27. Saul Bellow, *To Jerusalem and Back* (New York, 1976), p. 135.
28. *Ibid.*, p. 136.
29. See L. Poliakov, *History of Anti-Semitism*, I (New York, 1965), II (New York, 1973); Hannah Arendt, *The Origin of Totalitarianism* (New York, 1951); Arthur Hertzberg, *The French Enlightenment and the Jew* (New York, 1968); H. Valentin, *Anti-Semitism Historically and Critically Examined* (London, 1936); Koppel S. Pinson, ed., *Essays on Anti-Semitism* (New York, 1946).
30. William Brock, review of Rush Welter, *The Mind of America*, *Times Literary Supp.*, December 2, 1977, p. 1403.
31. *Goals for Americans*, The Report of the President's Commission on National Goals (New York, 1960), p. 1.
32. Arthur M. Schlesinger, "What Then Is the American, This New Man?" The essay was first published in *American Historical Review*, 48 (1942–1943), 225–244. It appears as the first chapter in the author's *Paths to the Present* (New York, 1949), pp. 1–22. Schlesinger's documentation of this essay is at pp. 278–283.

Notes to Chapter 1

1. *Crito* 50–51.
2. John Locke, *Second Treatise of Civil Government and A Letter Concerning Toleration*, ed. J. W. Gough (Oxford, 1947), sec. 58 of *Second Treatise*.
3. *Ibid.*, p. 143 (*Letter Concerning Toleration*).
4. *Pierce* v. *Society of Sisters*, 268 U.S. 510 (1925).
5. *Wisconsin* v. *Yoder*, 406 U.S. 205 (1972).
6. Only Article 21 may create a problem. It deals with what are generally considered political rights, such as participation in the government of one's country, and yet is written in terms of "everyone."
7. See "Adoption of the Bill of Rights" in M. R. Konvitz, *Fundamental Liberties of a Free People* (Ithaca, N.Y., 1957).
8. Job 13:15–16 (RSV).

9. Jerusalem Talmud, Nedarim, 9; Sifra, 89 b. Genesis Rabbah, Bereshet, xxiv, 7.

10. Matthew 22:32–40.

11. Genesis 5:1.

12. Hermann Cohen, *Religion of Reason out of the Sources of Judaism* (New York, 1972), p. 119.

13. This text is from Maimonides, *Code of Maimonides: Book of Judges*, trans. A. M. Hershman (New Haven, 1949), pp. 34–35. Cf. Mishnah, Sanhedrin, iv, 5.

14. Thomas Paine, *The Rights of Man* (Everyman ed.; London, 1915), p. 94. See also p. 98, note 1.

15. Deuteronomy Rabbah, Re'eh, iv, 4.

16. Thomas Jefferson in The Declaration of Independence.

17. Carl Becker, *The Heavenly City of the Eighteenth Century Philosophers* (New Haven, 1932), 15.

18. The Declaration of Independence.

Notes to Chapter 2

1. Menachem Elon, "Mishpat Ivri," 12 *Encyc. Judaica* 110, 115 ff.

2. *Ibid.*, p. 118.

3. Perry Miller, *Errand into the Wilderness* (Cambridge, 1956), ch. 1.

4. See, e.g., Hugh Davis Graham and Ted Robert Gurr, *Violence in America: Historical and Comparative Perspectives* (New York, 1969), a report submitted to the National Commission on the Causes and Prevention of Violence.

5. *Constitution of the United States, Analysis and Interpretation*, prepared by the Congressional Research Service, Library of Congress (Washington, D.C., 1973), p. xvii.

6. *Ibid.*, 1974 Supp., p. S126; also *Buckley* v. *Valeo*, 96 S.Ct. 612 (1976), making a total of 99 statutes.

7. *Dred Scott* v. *Sanford*, 19 How. 393 (1857). *Pollock* v. *Farmers' Loan & Trust Co.*, 157 U.S. 429 (1895); 158 U.S. 601 (1895); *Chisholm* v. *Georgia*, 2 Dall. 419 (1793).

8. *Engel* v. *Vitale*, 370 U.S. 421 (1962); *Abington School District* v. *Schempp* and *Murray* v. *Curlett*, 374 U.S. 203 (1963).

9. See M. R. Konvitz, *Expanding Liberties* (New York, 1966), p. 45. In 1973 the Dirksen Amendment was sponsored by Senator Richard S. Schweiker.

10. Chief Justice Hughes, in M. J. Pusey, *Charles Evans Hughes* (New York, 1951), p. 204.

11. Charles Warren, *The Supreme Court in United States History* (Boston, 1935), pp. 748–749.

12. Frankfurter, dissenting opinion, in *West Virginia State Board of Education* v. *Barnette*, 319 U.S. 624 (1943).

13. Kant, *Metaphysical Elements of Justice* (1797), p. 332.

14. *Plessy* v. *Ferguson*, 163 U.S. 537 (1896), introduced the "separate but equal" doctrine.

15. *Constitution of the United States, Analysis and Interpretation*, 1974 Supp., p. S.137, note 6, plus the decision in the shopping center case, *Hudgens* v. *NLRB*, 47 L.Ed. 2d 196 (1976), makes a total of 150 overruled cases.

16. *Law Week*, 44 (July 29, 1975), 3061.

17. Sifre, Numbers 15:31.

18. *The Fathers According to Rabbi Nathan*, trans. Judah Goldin (New Haven, 1955), p. 92.

19. Sanhedrin, 19a-b.

20. E. E. Urbach, *The Sages, Their Concepts and Beliefs*, trans. Israel Abrahams (Jerusalem, 1975), I, 572.

21. Maimonides, *Code of Maimonides: Book of Judges*, trans. A. M. Hershman (New Haven, 1949), pp. xvii, 8, 59, 61.

22. *Ibid.*, p. 212.

23. Sukkah, 30a.

24. Maimonides, *The Book of Judges*, p. 214.

25. *Marbury* v. *Madison*, 1 Cranch 137 (1803).

26. *Myers* v. *U.S.*, 272 U.S. 52 (1926).

27. *U.S.* v. *Curtiss-Wright Corp.*, 299 U.S. 304 (1936).

28. *Youngstown Sheet & Tube Co.* v. *Sawyer*, 343 U.S. 579 (1952).

29. *U.S.* v. *District Court for the Eastern District of Maryland*, 407 U.S. 297 (1972).

30. *U.S.* v. *Nixon*, 418 U.S. 683 (1974).

31. Ta'anit 23a (Henry Malter ed.; Philadelphia, 1928), p. 334.

32. Deuteronomy 17:18–20.

33. Emerson, *The Conduct of Life* (1860), ch. 1.

34. Mishnah, Berakoth, 9:3.

Notes to Chapter 3

1. See Henry A. Myers, *Are Men Equal?* (Ithaca, N.Y., 1945).

2. Genesis 1:1.

3. Psalms 5:4–5.

4. Isaiah 58:6–9.

5. Malachi 2:10.

6. Malachi 1:6.

7. Numbers Rabbah, Naso, x, 1.

8. Genesis 1:26.

9. Deuteronomy Rabbah, Re'eh, iv, 4.
10. Mishnah, Sanhedrin, iv, 5.
11. Midrash Psalms, on Psalm 117.
12. *Mekilta de-Rabbi Ishmael*, trans. J. Z. Lauterbach (Philadelphia, 1933), II, pp. 236–237.
13. Yalkut, on Isaiah 26, 2. Cf. C. G. Montefiore in *Judaism and Christianity*, ed. W. O. E. Oesterley (London, 1937), p. 116.
14. Tanna de Be Eliyyahu, 48. Yalkut, Lek Leka, 76.
15. Yalkut, Lek Leka, 74–75.
16. Jerusalem Talmud, Baba Mezia, ii, 5, 8c.
17. Babylonian Talmud, Abodah Zarah, 3a.
18. Leviticus Rabbah, Vayikrah, iii, 2.
19. Jerusalem Talmud, Dema'i, iv, 6, f. 24a.
20. Louis Finkelstein, Introduction to *Haggadah of Passover*, trans. Maurice Samuel (New York, 1942), p. xvii.
21. Isaiah 19:25.
22. Jeremiah 48:31.
23. Maimonides, Hilhot Teshubah, III, 5. Cf. Toisefta, Sanhedrin, xiii, 2.
24. Micah 6:6–8.
25. Jerusalem Talmud, Baba Mezia, ii, 5, 8c.
26. Tanhuma, Deuteronomy, Nizzabim.
27. Mishnah, Baba Kamma, viii, 6.
28. Numbers Rabbah, Naso, xi, 8.
29. Sifre, Numbers, Korah.
30. 10 *Encyc. Judaica* 1321–1322.
31. Cf. *Pirke Aboth*, vi, 4, 5.
32. Sifre, Deuteronomy, Ekeb.
33. *Authorized Daily Prayer Book*, trans. S. Singer (London, 1962), p. 290.
34. *Pirke Aboth*, iv, 7.
35. Ibid., ii, 9.
36. See E. E. Urbach, *The Sages: Their Concepts and Beliefs*, trans. Israel Abrahams (Jerusalem, 1975), I, pp. 601 ff.; Babylonian Talmud, Derek erez Zutta, iv, 2.
37. Babylonian Talmud, Nedarim, 62a.
38. Babylonian Talmud, Abodah Zara, 17b.
39. *Mekilta de-Rabbi Ishmael*, trans. J. Z. Lauterbach (Philadelphia, 1933), II, p. 103.
40. Deuteronomy 11:22.
41. *Pirke Aboth*, iii, 21.
42. Babylonian Talmud, Erubin, 13b.
43. Pesikta Rabbati 8a.
44. Babylonian Talmud, Gittin, 62a.
45. Maimonides, *Guide of the Perplexed*, III, ch. 26 ff.

46. Proverbs 25:21.
47. Leviticus 19:9; Deuteronomy 23:19.
48. Charles Foster Kent, *Social Teachings of the Prophets and Jesus* (New York, 1917), p. 11.
49. Deuteronomy 5:15.
50. *Haggadah of Passover*, p. 27.
51. Deuteronomy 5:9.
52. Deuteronomy 23:16–17.
53. Deuteronomy 23:25–26.
54. Deuteronomy 5:14.
55. Deuteronomy 24:14–15.
56. Deuteronomy 24:6, 10, 12–13.
57. Deuteronomy 15:1.
58. Deuteronomy 15:9.
59. Deuteronomy 15:10.
60. Deuteronomy 22:8.
61. Amos 2:6–8.
62. Amos 4:1–3.
63. Isaiah 5:8.
64. I Samuel 8:11–17.
65. I Kings 12:7.
66. II Samuel 20:1.
67. I Kings 21:27.
68. Tanhuma, Wayera, 49a.
69. Tanhuma, Bereshet, 6b.
70. Babylonian Talmud, Menahot, 29b.
71. Psalms 1:2.
72. Psalms 119:14, 16.
73. Deuteronomy Rabbah, Shofetim, v, 3.
74. Sifre, Deuteronomy, Ekeb, 84b.
75. Tanhuma, Bereshet, 6b.
76. Leviticus 25:42; Exodus 21:6; Babylonian Talmud, Kiddushin, 22b.

Notes to Chapter 4

1. Exodus 1:15–17.
2. Exodus 1:22.
3. I Samuel 22:17.
4. Daniel 3:16–18. The book was probably written in the second century B.C.E., though it purports to record events that were supposed to have happened in the sixth century B.C.E., and the history which is contained in the visions goes from the Babylonian period (sixth century) to the second century B.C.E. See *The Book of Daniel*, commentary

by Raymond Hammer (Cambridge Bible Commentary; Cambridge, 1976), pp. 3–6.

5. Daniel 6:1–17.
6. I Maccabees 1:62–63.
7. *Ibid.*, 2:20, 22.
8. *Ibid.*, 2:27.
9. II Maccabees 7:2.
10. *Third and Fourth Books of Maccabees*, ed. and trans. Moses Hadas (Dropsie University ed.; New York, 1953), 129.
11. Josephus, *The Jewish War* (Loeb Classical Library; London, 1927), II, 184–203.
12. Philo, *De Legatione ad Caium* (Loeb Classical Library; London, 1962), X, 232 ff.
13. Compare the Oedipus cycle in Greek drama for a similar feeling of revulsion against an incestuous act.
14. Babylonian Talmud, Sanhedrin, 74a.
15. In post-Talmudic Judaism, not all authorities agreed that the law imposed an absolute duty freely to choose martyrdom in view of the great degree of duress. They also stressed the question whether the cardinal sin was required to be committed publicly or secretly. The post-Talmudic discussions are not considered in this essay. See Samuel Belkin, *In His Image* (New York, n.d.), pp. 210, 211. Cf. David Daube, *Collaboration with Tyranny in Rabbinic Law* (New York, 1965), pp. 26, 27, 31, 35–36, 40, 83.
16. Konvitz, "Law and Morals in the Hebrew Scriptures, Plato, and Aristotle," *Conservative Judaism*, 23 (Winter 1969), 44.
17. Proverbs 7:3; Deuteronomy 30:14.
18. Jeremiah 31:32.
19. Deuteronomy 25:18.
20. Genesis 20:11.
21. Leviticus 5:21, 22.
22. Babylonian Talmud, Sanhedrin, 56a. Cf. Romans 2:14–15; Jubilees 7:22; Acts 15:20, 29.
23. Maimonides, Hilhot Yisodei Ha-Torah 5, 4. Cf. Belkin, *In His Image*, pp. 102–132.
24. Cf. Daube, *Collaboration*, pp. 99–100.
25. Cf. Yalkut, Lek Leka, sec. 76; Colossians 3:11.
26. R. J. Zvi Werblowsky, "The Concept of Conscience in Jewish Perspective," in *Conscience*, ed. Curatorium of C. G. Jung Institute, Zurich (Evanston, Ill., 1970), p. 81.
27. Job 27:6.
28. I Samuel 24:4–5.
29. Werblowsky, in *Conscience*, p. 90.
30. Philo, *De Decalogo* 82–91, trans. F. H. Colson (Cambridge, Mass., 1937), VII.

31. C. A. Pierce, *Conscience in the New Testament* (London, 1955), pp. 41, 46, 47. Cf. Josef Rudin, "A Catholic View of Conscience," in *Conscience*, ed. Curatorium of C. G. Jung Institute, Zurich (Evanston, Ill., 1970), pp. 142, 146.

32. Pierce, *Conscience in the New Testament*, p. 76.

33. I Corinthians 5.

34. Leviticus 18:7.

35. I Corinthians 5:5.

36. I Corinthians 6:9–12, 18.

37. C. S. C. Williams, "I and II Corinthians," *Peake's Commentary on the Bible* (London, 1962), p. 835b.

38. Pierce, *Conscience in the New Testament*, pp. 16, 57, 59.

39. *Ibid.*, p. 47.

40. Seneca, Letter 41, trans. Robin Campbell, in *Letters from a Stoic* (Penguin ed.; New York, 1969). The quotation within the passage is from Virgil, *Aeneid*, VIII:352. Cf. Rudin, "A Catholic View of Conscience," p. 142.

41. Romans 2:1–15.

42. I Corinthians 5.

43. Romans 1:18–21, 26–31.

44. Pierce, *Conscience in the New Testament*, p. 88, points out the sources of error in conscience noted by St. Paul.

45. Eric D'Arcy, *Conscience and Its Right to Freedom* (New York, 1961), pp. 5–8.

46. Pierce, *Conscience in the New Testament*, p. 114.

47. D'Arcy, *Conscience and Its Right to Freedom*, pp. 8–12.

48. *Ibid.*, pp. 11–12. Italics in original.

49. Plato, *Apology* 29C–30C, trans. H. N. Fowler (Loeb Classical Library; London, 1914).

50. *Ibid.*, 32D.

51. *Ibid.*, 31C–D.

52. *Ibid.*, 40B–C.

53. Epictetus, *Arrian's Discourses*, Bk. I, ch. I, 21–25, trans. W. A. Oldfather (Loeb Classical Library; London, 1925).

54. *Ibid.*, IV, ch. vii, 17–20.

55. Paul Tillich, *The Protestant Era*, trans. James Luther Adams (London, 1951), p. 154.

56. The anachronism in this statement of the case is, of course, recognized. The matter is presented not historically, but theoretically.

57. Cf. Adin Steinsaltz, *The Essential Talmud* (London, 1976), ch. 13.

58. See generally D'Arcy, *Conscience and Its Right to Freedom*.

59. *Ibid.*, p. 77.

60. *Ibid.*, p. 85.

61. *Ibid.*, pp. 100–101.
62. *Ibid.*, p. 113.
63. *Ibid.*, p. 125.
64. Tillich, *The Protestant Era*, pp. 155–157.
65. George H. Sabine, *A History of Political Theory* (3rd ed.; New York, 1961), 363.
66. John Calvin, *Institutes of a Christian Religion*, trans. John Allen (Philadelphia, 1936), II, Bk. IV, ch. 20, sec. xxiii.
67. *Ibid.*, sec. xxix, xxv.
68. *Ibid.*, sec. xxix.
69. *Ibid.*, sec. xxxii.
70. *Ibid.*, sec. xxxiii.
71. Calvin quotes Acts 5:29.
72. John Calvin, *Commentaries on the Book of the Prophet Daniel*, trans. Thomas Myers (Edinburgh, 1852–1853), I, 378, 381–384. Italics in original.
73. Calvin quotes Acts 5:29.
74. Plato, *Apology* 29d.
75. *Peake's Commentary on the Bible* (London, 1962), p. 892.
76. All except Luke, who was a Gentile, possibly converted by Paul.
77. See "The Cultural Background," by V. Tcherikover, in *The World History of the Jewish People: The Hellenistic Age* (New Brunswick, 1972), VI, ch. 2, bibliography, 347–348.
78. See Y. Arieli, *Individualism and Nationalism in American Ideology* (Cambridge, Mass. 1964), ch. 12.
79. Spinoza, *Tractatus Theologico-Politicus* (1670), in *The Chief Works of Benedict de Spinoza*, trans. R. H. Elwes (Dover ed.; New York, 1951), Preface.
80. The *Letter* was written in Latin in 1685/1686 and published in 1689. In the latter year an English edition appeared, translated by William Popple.
81. See W. K. Jordan, *The Development of Religious Toleration in England*, 4 vols. (London, 1932–1940).
82. John Locke, *Second Treatise of Civil Government and A Letter Concerning Toleration*, ed. J. W. Gough (Oxford, 1947), p. 123.
83. *Ibid.*, pp. 126–127, 135.
84. *Ibid.*, pp. 127–128, 141.
85. *Ibid.*, p. 128.
86. *Ibid.*, p. 129.
87. *Ibid.*, pp. 132–133.
88. *Ibid.*, p. 133, 135–136.
89. *Ibid.*, p. 143.
90. *Ibid.*, p. 146.

91. *Ibid.*, p. 150.

92. *Ibid.*, pp. 150–151.

93. *Ibid.*, pp. 147–148.

94. *Ibid.*, p. 153.

95. *Ibid.*

96. *Ibid.*

97. *Ibid.*, p. 154.

98. *Ibid.*, p. 155.

99. *Ibid.*, p. 156.

100. See Henry Kamen, *The Rise of Toleration* (London, 1967), p. 60.

101. See M. R. Konvitz, *Religious Liberty and Conscience* (New York, 1968), p. 75.

102. The establishment of the Anglican Church does not seem to be an exception, in any significant way, to the principles formulated by Locke. The accommodations between church and state in England reflect, on the whole, liberal Whig principles, though technically church and state are not altogether separate.

103. *Abington School District* v. *Schempp* and *Murray* v. *Curlett*, 374 U.S. 203 (1963); *Board of Education* v. *Allen*, 392 U.S. 236 (1968); *Lemon* v. *Kurtzman* and *Earley* v. *DiCenso*, 403 U.S. 602 (1971); *Tilton* v. *Richardson*, 403 U.S. 672 (1971).

104. Calvin, *Institutes of a Christian Religion*, p. 156.

105. Pierre Bayle, *Commentaire philosophique sur ces paroles de Jesus-Christ* 'contrains-les d'entrer,' 4 vols. (Amsterdam, 1686–1688). See Elizabeth Labrousse, "Religious Toleration," *Dict. Hist. of Ideas* (New York, 1973), IV, 112, 119.

106. Thomas More, *Utopia*, ed. Edward Surtz, in *Works of St. Thomas More* (Yale ed.; New Haven and London, 1964), p. 133.

107. *Ibid.*, p. 135. The person who did not believe in immortality and providence, while prohibited from airing his views in public, was to be allowed, and even encouraged, to discuss his religious views with "the priests and important personages."

108. See Kamen, *The Rise of Toleration*, p. 29.

109. Quoted in Wallace K. Ferguson, "The Attitude of Erasmus toward Toleration," in *Persecution and Liberty: Essays in Honor of George Lincoln Burr* (New York, 1931), pp. 171, 178.

110. *Ibid.*, pp. 176–177, 177–178.

111. *McGowan* v. *Maryland*, 366 U.S. 420 (1961).

112. *Braunfeld* v. *Brown*, 366 U.S. 599 (1961).

113. Cases cited in note 103, above.

114. *Braunfeld* v. *Brown*, 366 U.S. 599 (1961).

115. *Sherbert* v. *Verner*, 374 U.S. 398 (1963).

116. *Wisconsin* v. *Yoder*, 406 U.S. 205, 215 (1972).

117. *Ibid.*, p. 230; cf. pp. 233–234.

Notes to Chapter 5

1. Exodus 24:7.

2. George Foot Moore, *Judaism in the First Centuries of the Christian Era* (Cambridge, Mass., 1927), II, 208, 219.

3. The first prayer is at the beginning of the morning service; it avows the purity of the soul as given by the Creator. It may have been inspired by a wish to counter the Christian dogma of original sin. See Babylonian Talmud, Berakoth, 60b. The second prayer comes at the end of the Amidah; it was written by Mar bar Rabina and is a prayer for the strengthening of one's humility and other ethical qualities. See *ibid.*, at 17a.

4. Martin Buber, *The Ten Rungs* (New York, 1947), p. 31.

5. Exodus 14:30–15:18.

6. Moore, *Judaism in the First Centuries*, II, 222.

7. Judah Halevi, *Kitab al Khazari*, trans. H. Hirschfeld (New York, 1927), pp. 155–157.

8. Joseph Albo, *Sefer Ha-Ikkarim*, ed. Isaac Husik (Philadelphia, 1930), IV, ch. 21, 192.

9. Babylonian Talmud, Berakoth, 29b–30a.

10. F. Tonnies, *Gemeinschaft und Gesellschaft* (1877), trans. Charles P. Loomis, in *Community and Society* (East Lansing, Michigan, 1957).

11. *Shohet*, a ritual slaughterer; *mohel*, religious functionary who performs circumcisions; *mikvah*, a ritual bath.

12. *Hevrah kadishah*, religious burial society.

13. Babylonian Talmud, Sanhedrin, 27b; Shebi'it, 39a.

14. Babylonian Talmud, Shabbat, 54b.

15. *Mekilta de-Rabbi Ishmael*, trans. J. Z. Lauterbach (Philadelphia, 1933), II, 205–206.

16. Maimonides, Code of Maimonides, Tshubah III, 4. Cf. Babylonian Talmud, Rosh Hashonah, 17a.

17. Babylonian Talmud, Sukkah, 53a.

18. Ezekiel 18:20.

19. In 1968 Benjamin Shalit, a lieutenant commander in the Israel navy, requested that his two children, born of a non-Jewish mother, be registered on their identity cards as Jews. The Ministry of the Interior refused. In 1970 the Supreme Court, by 5-4 vote, held that the registrar was bound to accept the designation offered by the registrant. The decision raised strong public protest, and subsequently the law was changed to accept only those born of Jewish mothers or converted to Judaism. 10 *Encyc. Judaica* 23–24.

20. Oswald Rufeisen, born a Jew and a convert to Catholicism, claimed that he qualified as a Jew under Israel's Law of Return and

could, therefore, claim Israeli citizenship, not as a non-Jewish immigrant but simply as a Jew, without regard to his religious beliefs. In 1966 the Supreme Court of Israel decided against Rufeisen, who called himself Brother Daniel, despite his valid halakhic claims to Jewish status, on the ground that he had chosen to remove himself by conversion from the history and destiny of the Jewish people. 3 *Encyc. Judaica* 209 ff.; 10 *Encyc. Judaica*, 63.

21. But it should be noted that the traditionalist, as the Brother Daniel case showed, would draw the line at apostasy. Despite the fact that the Halakhah was in Brother Daniel's favor, there was no public outcry against the decision of the Supreme Court against his claim of continuing to be a Jew under the Law of Return, adopted in 1950, which declares that every Jew has the right to settle in Israel; under the Nationality Law of 1952, every settler (*oleh*) under the Law of Return is an Israeli national.

22. The exceptions related to the problem of public funds for Jewish all-day schools, "parochaid." As the financial strain has intensified, supporters of these schools have joined Catholic forces in their contention that government aid for religious schools is no breach of the wall of separation of church and state and that a denial of such aid is an infringement of religious liberty. The overwhelming majority of Jewish organizations have, however, consistently opposed such financial aid by government.

23. Babylonian Talmud, Erubin, 13b.

24. Leviticus 20:23.

25. William James, "On a Certain Blindness in Human Beings," in *Talks to Teachers on Psychology* (New York, 1915), p. 229.

26. Solomon Schechter, *Studies in Judaism* (1st ser.; Philadelphia, repr. 1938), Preface, xxi.

27. See note 21 above for the Law of Return.

28. See quotation from Jefferson in C. H. Moehlman, *The Wall of Separation between Church and State* (Boston, 1951), pp. 77–78. Cf. M. R. Konvitz, *Fundamental Liberties of a Free People* (Ithaca, N.Y., 1957), p. 280.

29. James, "On a Certain Blindness," p. 264.

30. See *Pirke Aboth*, vi, 21.

Notes to Chapter 6

1. S. M. Dubnow, *History of the Jews in Russia and Poland* (Philadelphia, 1916), II, 256, 257; III, 89, 102.

2. *Ibid..* III, 115–116.

3. Haim Hillel Ben-Sasson, "Self-Defense," 14 *Encyc. Judaica* 1123–1127.

4. Hobbes, *Leviathan*, Pt. 1, ch. 13.

5. *U.S. News and World Report*, Feb. 4, 1974, pp. 40–42.

6. Dubnow, *History of the Jews*, III, 111–112, 131–146.

7. *Ibid.*, III, 146–48.

8. Isaac Levitats, "Minority Rights," 12 *Encyc. Judaica* 43.

9. Edgar Mortara, a Jewish child, was abducted by papal authorities in Bologna.

10. *The Pursuit of Equality: A Half Century with the American Jewish Committee (New York,* 1957), p. 17.

11. Naomi W. Cohen, *Not Free to Desist: The American Jewish Committee 1906–1966* (Philadelphia, 1972), p. 66.

12. *The Pursuit of Equality*, pp. 19–20.

13. Naomi W. Cohen, *Not Free to Desist*, p. 384.

14. *Ibid.*, p. 29.

15. Significantly, the American Jewish Committee refused to act on behalf of Frank, but Louis Marshall individually served as his counsel.

16. Naomi W. Cohen, *Not Free to Desist*, pp. 385–386; cf. 344, 351.

17. M. R. Konvitz, ed., *Law and Social Action: Selected Essays of Alexander H. Pekelis* (Ithaca, N.Y., 1950), pp. 218 ff.

18. *Ibid.*, p. 242 (italics in original).

19. Rufus Learsi, *The Jews in America: A History* (New York, 1954), p. 75.

20. *Ibid.*, pp. 84–85, 89, 132.

21. *Ibid.*, p. 213.

22. Italics supplied.

Notes to Chapter 7

1. Letter to James Madison, Aug. 30, 1823; see Dumas Malone, *Jefferson the Virginian* (Boston, 1948), p. 226.

2. Charles M. Wiltse, *The Jeffersonian Tradition in American Democracy* (Chapel Hill, 1935), p. 70.

3. Howard Mumford Jones, *The Pursuit of Happiness* (Cambridge, Mass., 1953), p. 86.

4. Carl Becker, *The Declaration of Independence* (New York, 1922, repr. 1942), p. 79.

5. Quoted by Gilbert Chinard, *Thomas Jefferson: The Apostle of Americanism* (Ann Arbor, Mich., 1957), p. 71.

6. *Ibid.*, 73; Malone, *Jefferson the Virginian*, p. 220.

7. Chinard, *Thomas Jefferson: The Apostle of Americanism*, p. 73.

8. *Ibid.*, p. 74; Malone, *Jefferson the Virginian*, p. 221; Ralph Barton Perry, *Puritanism and Democracy* (New York, 1944), p. 187.

9. John Clive, *Macaulay: The Shaping of the Historian* (New York, 1973), p. 290.

10. John Locke, *Second Treatise of Civil Government*, ch. IX, sec. 123.

11. *Ibid.*, ch. XI, sec. 137.

12. W. J. Bate, *John Keats* (New York, 1963), pp. 516 ff.

13. M. R. Konvitz, "Dewey's Revision of Jefferson," in Sidney Hook, ed., *John Dewey: Philosopher of Science and Freedom* (New York, 1950).

14. Adrienne Koch, *Philosophy of Thomas Jefferson* (New York, 1943), p. 175.

15. Wiltse, *The Jeffersonian Tradition*, pp. 73–74.

16. Chinard, *Thomas Jefferson: The Apostle of Americanism*, pp. 80–82.

17. Adrienne Koch and William Peden, eds., *The Life and Selected Writings of Thomas Jefferson* (New York, 1944), pp. 464, 466.

18. By terms of the Constitution nine states were sufficient for its establishment. New Hampshire, on June 21, 1788, became the ninth state to ratify. But as a practical matter it was recognized that ratification by Virginia and New York was indispensable. Virginia ratified on June 25, 1788, and New York on July 26, 1788. The new and first Congress convened on March 4, 1789. The Bill of Rights was adopted by Congress on Sept. 24, 1789, and was ratified on Dec. 15, 1791.

19. Letter to Madison, Dec. 10, 1787, in Adrienne Koch, ed., *Jefferson* (Englewood, N.J., 1971), pp. 37, 38.

20. Locke, *Second Treatise*, ch. XI, sec. 135.

21. See generally Herbert L. Ganther, "Jefferson's 'Pursuit of Happiness' and Some Forgotten Men," *William & Mary College Q.*, 2d Series, 16 (no. 3; July 1936), 422; second part, at 558.

22. Locke, *An Essay Concerning Human Understanding* (Everyman ed.; New York, 1912), I, Bk. II, ch. XXI, p. 215.

23. Herman Melville, *Hawthorne and His Mosses*.

24. Leonard Woolf, *After the Deluge: A Study of Communal Psychology* (London, 1931), I, 191–192.

25. Cf. Universal Declaration of Human Rights, of the United Nations Assembly, adopted Dec. 10, 1948.

26. David Cecil, *Library Looking-Glass* (London, 1975), p. 113.

27. Cf. *ibid.*, p. 133, Walter DeLaMare on Robert Bridges.

28. Deuteronomy 26:11.

29. *Ibid.*, 28:47.

30. *Ibid.*, 14:26.

31. See M. R. Konvitz, "Judaism and the Pursuit of Happiness," in *The Menorah Treasury*, ed. Leo W. Schwarz (Philadelphia, 1964), p. 881; reprinted in *Judaism and Human Rights*, ed. M. R. Konvitz (New York, 1972), p. 216.

32. Deuteronomy 11:8–15.

33. *Ibid.*, 30:9.

34. Isaiah, ch. 65.

35. Genesis Rabbah, Bereshet, ix, 7.

36. E. La B. Cherbonnier, *Hardness of Heart* (New York, 1955).

37. Maimonides, *Shemonah Perakim*, trans. by J. I. Gorfinkle, *The Eight Chapters of Maimonides on Ethics* (New York, 1912), p. 63; translation in text is by L. E. Goodman, *Rambam: Readings in Philosophy of Moses Maimonides* (New York, 1976), 229.

38. Emerson's essay on "Civilization," in his volume *Society and Solitude* (1870).

INDEX

Judaism and the
American Idea

Designed by Guy Fleming
Composed by G&S Typesetters, Inc.,
in 10 point VIP Primer, 3 points leaded,
with display lines in Photo Typositor Bauer Bodoni
Printed offset by Vail-Ballou Press, Inc.
Bound by Vail-Ballou Press
in Joanna book cloth
and stamped in All Purpose foil.

Library of Congress Cataloging in Publication Data
(For library cataloging puposes only)
Konvitz, Milton Ridvas, 1908–
  Judaism and the American idea.

  Includes bibliographical references and index.
  1. Civil rights—United States—History—Addresses, essays, lectures.
2. Political science—United States—History—Addresses, essays, lectures.
3. Judaism—History—To 70 A.D.—Addresses, essays, lectures,.   4. Judaism
and democracy—Addresses, essays, lectures.   5. Bible—Political science—
Addresses, essays, lectures.   I. Title.
JC599.U5K63   323.4'01   78-58028
ISBN 0-8014-1181-5